A Kid's Guide to
WASHINGTON, D.C.

HARCOURT, INC.

ORLANDO AUSTIN NEW YORK SAN DIEGO LONDON

www.hmhco.com

Written by Diane C. Clark
Revised and updated by Miriam Chernick
Illustrations and maps by Richard E. Brown

Library of Congress Cataloging-in-Publication Data
Clark, Diane C.
A kid's guide to Washington, D.C./written by Diane C. Clark; illustrations and maps by
Richard E. Brown—Rev. and updated ed./by Miriam Chernick.
p. cm.
Includes index.
1. Washington (D.C.)—Guidebooks—Juvenile literature. 2. Children—Travel—Washington
(D.C.)—Guidebooks—Juvenile literature. 3. Games—Juvenile literature. 4. Puzzles—Juvenile
literature. I. Brown, Richard E. (Richard Eric), 1946- ill. II. Chernick, Miriam. III. Title.
F192.3.C53 2008
2007015509
ISBN 978-0-15-206125-8

Text set in NeutraText Book
Designed by Kristine Brogno

SCP 12 11
4500556368

Manufactured in China

Contents

How to Use This Book

Are you planning a visit to Washington, D.C.?
Read this book before you leave, then carry it with you
while you're there. It will help you choose where you want
to go each day. But don't just read this book!
Use the maps: Try to figure out
where you are and where you
want to go. There are games
and puzzles all through the
book for you to do while riding
in a car or plane, waiting to
eat, or just hanging around
waiting for the grown-ups to get going!

The introduction to the book tells you things like
what the weather is like in Washington (so you'll
know what kind of clothes to bring), the different
ways to travel into the city, and how to get around
once you're there.

Following this introduction are chapters about the
history, government, people, and animals that make
Washington, D.C., such an interesting place to visit.
There are descriptions of places to visit, tips on where
to eat, and suggestions on where to get the most
unusual souvenirs.

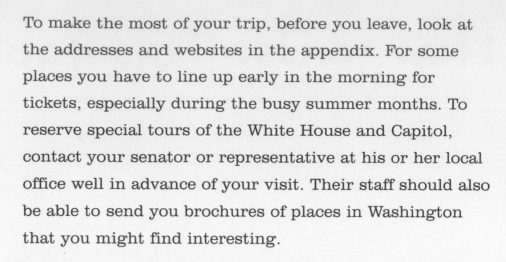

To make the most of your trip, before you leave, look at the addresses and websites in the appendix. For some places you have to line up early in the morning for tickets, especially during the busy summer months. To reserve special tours of the White House and Capitol, contact your senator or representative at his or her local office well in advance of your visit. Their staff should also be able to send you brochures of places in Washington that you might find interesting.

The web addresses in the appendix will also help you research details such as handicap accessibility, admission fees, seasonal changes in hours, or closures for security reasons.

Following the appendix, you'll discover a number of games you can play in the car and answers to the puzzles in this book. In the very back is an index, where you can look up the page numbers for specific places you want to read about.

Security has been increased since 9/11, so once you're in Washington, be prepared to walk through metal detectors and have your bag searched. Be flexible in your planning as some locations close on short notice.

Be sure to stop by information desks to ask about programs for kids. Most of the museums and galleries have special brochures, tours, and activities that will make your visit more fun.

United States of America

Washington, D.C.

And pick up some of the publications that list special events while you're in town. The *Washington Post* is a wonderful source of information, particularly on Fridays with the newspaper's *Weekend* section. Another helpful resource is *Washington Parent,* a free publication that includes a monthly calendar with area activities for families.

Whatever you end up doing, feel free to write your impressions in this book. Color and draw wherever there's room, in the margins or on top of the pictures already here. Write about the places you have seen, what you liked best or least about a place. Write whatever you want!

It might also be fun to keep a separate journal about your trip, including interesting or funny things that happened to you and your family. Save your ticket stubs, brochures, and menus. When you get home, make a scrapbook of all your mementos, photos, and illustrations. It's a great way to remember your trip when it's over.

Today we went to the washington monument. It was neat. The line was long. It took about an hour to get on the elevator, but the view from the top was awesome.

Welcome to Washington, D.C.

Can you locate Washington, D.C., on a map of the United States? It's that diamond-shaped dot on the East Coast bordered by Maryland on the north and Virginia on the south.

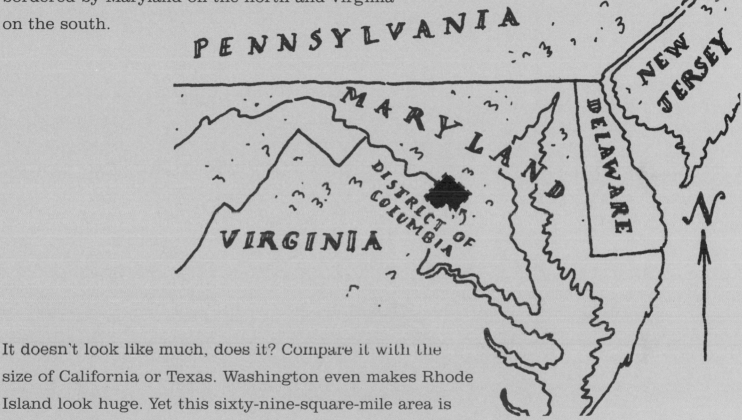

It doesn't look like much, does it? Compare it with the size of California or Texas. Washington even makes Rhode Island look huge. Yet this sixty-nine-square-mile area is the capital of the country, the headquarters of the federal government, and the home of embassies that represent countries all over the world. Every year Washington is visited by royalty, heads of government, business leaders, and seventeen million tourists.

A trip to Washington, D.C., has lots of surprises and adventures in store—things that you can't see or do anywhere else in the world. You'll have the chance to witness government in action and learn how bills, such as setting the highway speed limit or the amount of taxes an American family pays, are passed. You may even meet your own senator.

You'll find out where the president and first lady live. And you'll see the highest court in the nation and the largest library in the world.

If you're a fan of James Bond, you'll enjoy learning that there are more spies in Washington than in any other city on Earth. You'll see a real-life spying device—a camera hidden in a button—and get the chance to decipher a secret code.

And money—you'll see more money than Uncle Scrooge could hoard in a lifetime when you visit a printing plant that manufactures the country's bills.

You'll also get a chance to step back in history. You can visit places where time stands still; places where colonial families and farmers till soil and churn butter just like they did 400 years ago. You can even eat gingerbread made from the recipe of George Washington's mother, Mary Washington. You'll see a replica of George Washington's teeth and solve the mystery question: Were they really made of wood?

You can see the Declaration of Independence, the gun that killed Abraham Lincoln, a fence made from Civil War muskets, cannonballs still lodged in houses, and the church pew where Civil War general Robert E. Lee sat.

And that's just the beginning. There are many other thrilling sights: the ruby slippers worn by Dorothy in *The Wizard of Oz,* Thomas Edison's lightbulb, and Thomas Jefferson's bible. Or how about the largest blue diamond in the world, a real dinosaur egg, or a human hair ball pulled out of a young girl's stomach?

Did You Know?

July 4, 1776, is known as the date of the signing of the Declaration of Independence. This isn't quite true. It was adopted on July 4, but it wasn't actually signed until August 2, 1776.

Do you want to see the *Kitty Hawk Flyer,* the plane that flew Orville and Wilbur Wright into the history books? Or walk through *Skylab*? Or touch a piece of the moon? You can do all these things on your trip, if time allows.

Did You Know?

Washington, D.C., was not always the name of the capital. It was originally called Federal City.

• • •

George Washington never wanted to name the new capital Washington, out of modesty.

• • •

In 1912, the city of Tokyo, Japan, gave three thousand cherry trees, or *sakura,* to the United States. That's where Washington's cherry blossoms originate.

Test ★ Yourself

Q: What city was the first temporary capital of the United States?

A: Philadelphia.

But first, here's a little more information about Washington, D.C.

Where do you think they got the name Washington? If you said from George Washington, the first president of the United States, you were right.

But do you know what "D.C." stands for? It means District of Columbia, named for Christopher Columbus. Washington, D.C., is not a state. People who live in Washington, D.C., do not have legislators in Congress who can vote on their behalf. Washingtonians have one delegate who can speak for them, but that delegate can only vote in smaller committee meetings.

Look closely at the Washington, D.C., license plate for an expression of the locals' discontent: "Taxation without Representation." For many years, residents of Washington, D.C., weren't even allowed to vote for president. But in 1964 that changed, and now they can.

Packing for the Trip

What to bring to Washington, D.C., depends on the season. In winter it doesn't snow a lot, but the weather is cold and rainy. You'll need warm pants, sweaters, a coat, gloves, a scarf, and a hat. Since snow quickly turns to slush, waterproof boots and comfortable shoes for sightseeing are a must.

Washington's spring season lives up to the saying "April showers bring May flowers." Be sure to take an umbrella and a raincoat. But even if it sprinkles, Washington is at its most beautiful in spring, with the cherry trees, forsythia, and azaleas in full bloom.

Summers are hot and muggy, with temperatures in the 90s. It's T-shirt and shorts time, but remember to bring along a sweater for air-conditioned museums and restaurants.

Fall is crisp and cool. Bring warm clothes—and yes, an umbrella. Washington often gets autumn showers, too.

Getting There

There are lots of ways to get to Washington, D.C.: car, bus, train, or plane.

Flying is very popular. More than thirty-three million people fly into one of the area's three airports each year. The closest is Ronald Reagan Washington National Airport, just fifteen minutes from the White House and across the Potomac River, which separates Washington from Virginia. Try to grab a window seat, because as you land you'll get a great view of the Capitol, the Washington Monument, and the Lincoln and Jefferson memorials.

Washington Dulles International Airport, also in Virginia, is about forty-five minutes from downtown Washington, D.C. You'll fly in over trees and fields, but imagine what the area might have looked like in 1862. In August and September of that year, the land surrounding Dulles was a battleground in the second Bull Run clash of the Civil War.

The third airport is Baltimore-Washington International Airport, about fifty minutes north of the city, in Maryland.

Driving into Washington—whether from the north, south, or west—takes you past historic towns and battle sites.

If you're arriving from Richmond, Virginia, you'll pass by the **National Museum of the Marine Corps** next to the Marine Corps base in Quantico. This new museum opened in November 2006 as a tribute to U.S. Marines and is especially popular with visitors. The soaring design of the 118,000-square-foot museum evokes the image of the flag-raisers of Iwo Jima and houses interactive exhibits and artifacts such as tanks, aircraft, landing craft, and weapons. The history you'll experience through the eyes of those dedicated Marines who fought for our country will make you want to shout "Ooh-Rah!"

Driving from the north brings you through Baltimore, Maryland, a major East Coast port city. Several miles to the east is the Chesapeake Bay—an arm of water jutting in from the Atlantic Ocean. Although much of the sea life has been depleted by pollution, many fishermen still make their living gathering clams, oysters, and the blue crabs for which Maryland is famous.

Just before entering Washington on the Baltimore-Washington Parkway, you'll pass the **NASA Goddard Space Flight Center**. Here you'll find an amazing collection of rockets and satellites.

If you're arriving from the west, you could make a stop at **Luray Caverns** in Virginia. Stroll through cave after cave to view unusual rock formations. Some resemble fried eggs sunny-side up, strips of bacon, and Turkish towels. These caverns, tunneling 164 feet underground, are the largest in the eastern United States.

Whatever direction you're coming from, if it's by car, you're likely to drive at least a few miles on Interstate 495, or the Capital Beltway, a highway that almost completely circles the city. This is where the phrase "Inside the Beltway" comes from. It refers to the political happenings, real or assumed, in the federal government.

If your family decides to ride the train into Washington, you'll arrive at **Union Station,** a grand old building completed in 1907. At the time it was built, Union Station was the largest train station in the world. Today, it is not only a transportation hub but a great place to find all kinds of shopping and restaurants—and you can even catch a movie here.

Did You Know?

More than twenty-nine million people come through Union Station each year, making it the most visited site in all of Washington, D.C.

Whether by car, train, bus, or plane, there is a route you have to follow to reach Washington, D.C. Color in the state where you live and draw a line tracing your path from home to Washington on the map on page 7.

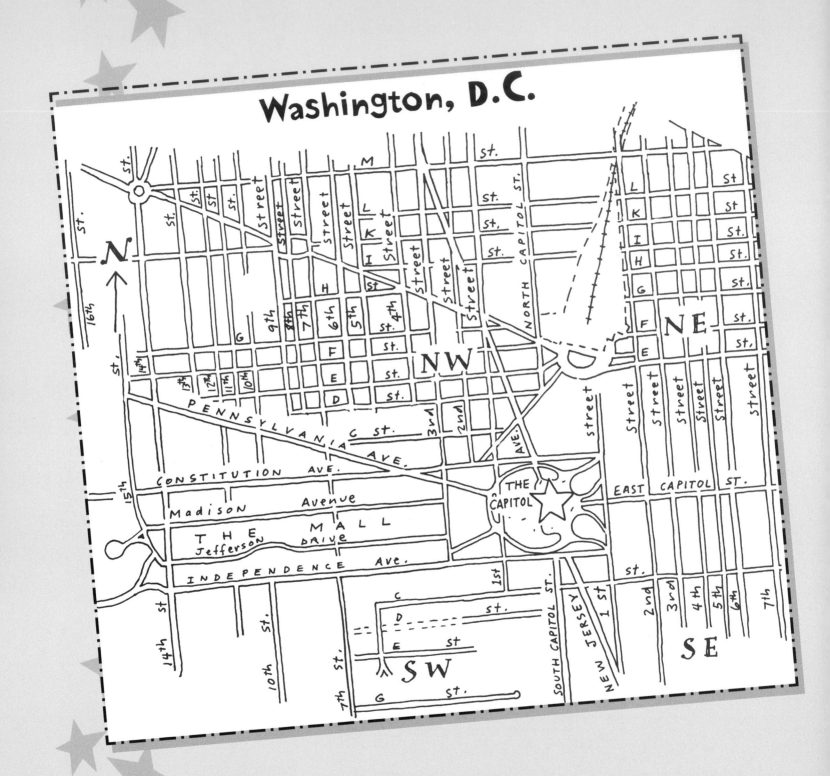

Washington, D.C.

Getting Around

Finding your way around many cities is a nightmare, but Washington, D.C., was designed to be a snap. The Capitol is anchored like the hub of a wheel. Four spokes come out from the Capitol at right angles, dividing the city into four sections, or quadrants. The spokes are North Capitol Street, South Capitol Street, East Capitol Street, and on the west side of the building, instead of an actual street, the grassy National Mall (the area between the Washington Monument and the U.S. Capitol). The four sections of Washington are called Northwest (NW), Northeast (NE), Southwest (SW), and Southeast (SE). You can always tell what section of the city you're in by looking at a street sign. All street names are followed by one of these abbreviations.

Within each of these four areas the roads running north and south are numbered—1st Street, 2nd Street, 3rd Street, and so on. The roads running east and west are named after letters of the alphabet—C Street, D Street, E Street, and so forth. There are no A or B Streets because A Street became the Mall and East Capitol Street, and B Street was renamed Constitution Avenue on the north side of the Mall and Independence Avenue on the south side.

After the letters are used up, street names become words in alphabetical order, starting with one-syllable words, then two, then three syllables. So about six miles away

19

from the Capitol, you'll find Albemarle Street, Brandywine Street, Chesapeake Street, and so on. This alphabetical lineup keeps repeating itself until it reaches the Maryland and Virginia borders.

Exceptions to the rule are the major avenues that run diagonally across the district and are named after states such as Massachusetts, Connecticut, and Pennsylvania.

Knowing the layout of the city makes it easy to figure out where you are and how to get where you're going. For instance, if you are at 14th and E Streets, NW, and need to go to the Capitol, you have to walk fourteen blocks to the east and four blocks to the south. If you are at 15th and M Streets and need to get to 12th and K Streets, you go two blocks down to K Street and three blocks over to 12th Street.

It's amazing to think that this simple street plot was designed about 200 years ago by Washington's first city planner, Frenchman Pierre L'Enfant. But it's not a perfect grid because L'Enfant's design wasn't completed until long after his death and more streets had to be added as the city grew.

Even though streets are easy to locate, you may not want to drive in Washington because parking is hard to find. The best way to get around is by taxi, bus, or subway.

Did You Know?

Pierre L'Enfant, whose clever Washington, D.C., street plan is praised today, died in poverty in 1825.

L ST. 28th ST.

Taxis in Washington do not have meters. You are charged by zone. Every time you pass from one zone to another, the fare goes up. It also increases at rush hour, during stormy weather, and if you have extra people. A map of the zones is in the back of each cab.

You can go almost anywhere in Washington by bus. Bus maps are available at all Metrorail stations, or you can call or look online for **Metrobus** information. Even if you aren't prepared, bus drivers are friendly and can point you in the right direction.

The **Tourmobile** is a special bus that runs continuously around the Mall and into Virginia, stopping at top sightseeing attractions along the way. Invest in an all-day ticket, which allows you to get on and off the Tourmobile at preset bus stops as often as you like.

Here's a problem for you to solve on your own: If you are at Third and Constitution, NW, and want to go to Third and F Street, NW, how many blocks will you have to travel? (You can use the map on page 18 to figure this out.)

(Answer on page 147)

Did You Know?

The Wheaton Metro Station has the longest escalator in the Western Hemisphere: 508 feet (almost two football fields).

TOURS

WMATA Photograph by Larry Levine

More popular than the bus is **Metrorail**. This subway system opened in 1976 and is one of the fastest and easiest ways to get around. Each person needs a fare card to enter and exit. You can find out how much your fare is by looking at the map near the ticket machines. Insert your money into a ticket machine and your ticket will come out. Using Metrorail can be confusing at first. If you have any questions, ask one of the station managers in the glass booth nearby.

Subway lines are distinguished by their color—red, orange, blue, green, and yellow. To catch your train, follow the sign and color announcing the final destination of the line you want to take. Be sure to check the front and sides of the train to make certain it's the right color, because sometimes two lines stop at the same place.

If you head in the wrong direction, don't panic. Just get off at the next stop and hop on a train coming back the other way. Metrorail trains run from 5:00 A.M. Monday through Friday and from 7:00 A.M. on Saturday and Sunday. Metrorail closes at midnight Sunday through Thursday, and at 3:00 A.M. Saturday and Sunday. There's usually no more than a fifteen-minute wait.

Now you're all set to find your way around the city. But first you need to know a little more about this unusual area and how it came to be.

A Brief History

Way Back When

When European explorers first came to what is now Washington, D.C., they were met by Native Americans who lived in small villages scattered along the rivers and in the forests. The Europeans traded with the native people, who taught them a lot about how to live in this strange "new" land. The settlers learned how to fish, and, more important, how to grow and use corn, a basic Native American food.

With the arrival of the Europeans who started to settle in this area came diseases unknown to the locals. Many died from these foreign illnesses. Others, persecuted by the Europeans, moved west. By the 1600s there were very few local Native Americans left here.

Colonial America

The settlers divided the land into farms, both large and small. Because there were no cities, the really big farms became centers of activity. These large farms were called "plantations," and the rich landowners brought in slaves from Africa to work in their fields. The plantation owners lived comfortably, but small farmers, craftsmen, laborers, servants, and slaves had to work hard just to survive.

Life in colonial America was far different from life today. There was no electricity or plumbing. Many homes didn't even have kitchens. Cooking was often done in a separate building because of the danger of fire. The colonists ate simple food, and corn became a major part of their diet. They also hunted and ate rabbit, deer, squirrel, and pigeon. Because there was little milk, kids had to drink hard cider, beer, and wine—even for breakfast!

Did You Know?

In colonial times, boys wore dresses and petticoats until age four or five. Then they switched to adult-style clothes.

• • •

Women almost always wore a hat—even in the house. Men usually shaved off their hair and wore a powdered wig.

Very few children went to school back then. If a family was rich, they paid a teacher to live in the house and teach the kids at home. Sometimes several farm families got together, built a small schoolhouse, and hired a teacher. Boys went to school longer than girls because girls were expected to get married at age sixteen or seventeen, raise a family, and keep house.

Because coins were scarce, the colonists often used tobacco leaves grown on their farms for money. They paid the doctor or bought a new wagon with tobacco. They even paid their taxes with tobacco!

Revolutionary Times

The colonists, under the rule of England, became angry at having to pay taxes to a government clear across the Atlantic Ocean. They started to protest British rule. That was the beginning of the American Revolution. In 1776, the thirteen colonies declared their independence from England, and the United States was born.

Realizing that they needed a new government to take the place of the old, a group of men got together and wrote the Constitution, one of the nation's most important documents. In it they set down a framework for government that is still used today. The colonists chose George Washington, the general who led them in the American Revolution, as their first president.

After the war, the lawmakers who wrote the Constitution decided this new country needed a permanent home for its government. President George Washington selected a site along the Potomac River that was partly in Maryland and partly in Virginia. And in 1790, the District of Columbia came into being.

Construction of the new city began. French-born engineer Pierre L'Enfant agreed to design Federal City (which Washington, D.C., was originally called). He chose a hill overlooking the area as the site of the Capitol Building. His plans were to create a magnificent city that would make the American people proud. L'Enfant's design was very grand, but his temper got in the way and he was fired.

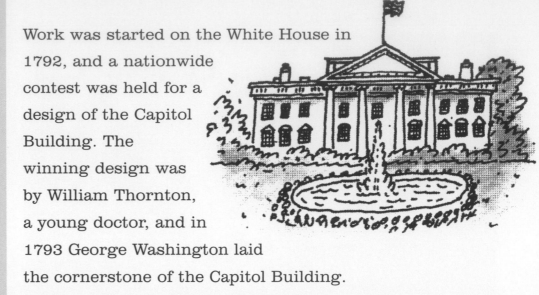

Work was started on the White House in 1792, and a nationwide contest was held for a design of the Capitol Building. The winning design was by William Thornton, a young doctor, and in 1793 George Washington laid the cornerstone of the Capitol Building.

The War of 1812 and Beyond

It wasn't very long after the Capitol, the White House, and other new buildings were built that the new nation went to war again with Great Britain. And this time the enemy soldiers set a lot of government buildings on fire. If not for a rainstorm, the buildings would have been completely destroyed. After the rain, there was a windstorm that was so violent that several houses caved in, cannons were blown over, and thirty British soldiers were killed. The British, who were losing the war, fled and the city began rebuilding.

History Crossword Puzzle

1. Colonial men shaved their heads and wore these kinds of wigs.
2. Colonial boys wore these until they were 4 or 5 years old.
3. Students used to write with lumps of this.
4. Native Americans taught the colonists how to grow and eat this.
5. Colonists were angry at having to pay taxes to this country.
6. The framework of the U.S. government was set down in this document.
7. Colonists used it for money.
8. The North wanted to free them; the South didn't.
9. Pierre L'Enfant chose a hill for its site.

(Answers on page 147)

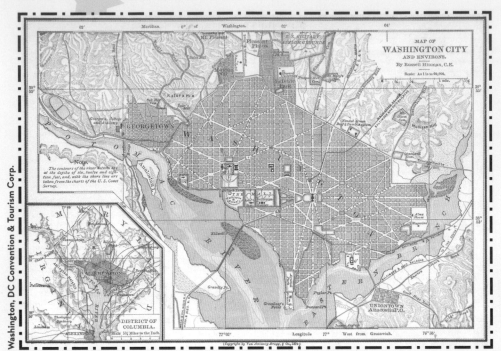

The next major crisis for the growing nation was the Civil War. This war pitted the North, which wanted to free the slaves, against the South, which needed the slave labor to harvest its crops. The nation's capital became a headquarters for Northern troops. The Capitol Building was turned into a food warehouse, bakery, and sleeping quarters for soldiers. Thousands of slaves fled their plantations and came to Washington to be free. Many freed slaves put down roots, bought land, and worked hard to educate their children.

Over the years, due to segregation, the African American community looked inward for support and leadership. And by the end of World War II, Washington had a higher proportion of African American college graduates than anywhere else in the United States. The area around U Street became a center for artists such as poet Langston Hughes and musician Duke Ellington. Until the late '60s, when U Street became more known as the birthplace of the 1968 riots, Washington had a vibrant and self-sufficient African American community.

Eventually, many residents moved away. But to this day, African Americans make up more than half of the population of Washington, D.C.

The Nation's Capital Today

When the Civil War was over in 1865, the city once again patched up its damage and continued to grow as the country's capital. From 8,000 residents in 1800, D.C.'s population climbed to about 800,000 in the 1950s. With the appeal of suburban living, Washington's population began to slowly decrease to fewer than 600,000 today. The larger Washington metropolitan area, which includes parts of Virginia and Maryland, has a population of almost six million.

National Park Service

There aren't just Americans in Washington, D.C. There are people from all over the world. Almost every country has a representative in Washington, in addition to many foreign students and businesspeople. There are important schools for government and international politics, and a great deal of scientific research is done in this city. As you can probably guess, Washington has more news reporters than anywhere else, too. Newpapers and radio and television stations gather and send news all over the world from the nation's capital.

Washington, D.C., is a large and important city, but it doesn't look like most American cities. Why? Look at the buildings. There are no skyscrapers! That's because there's a rule against a building being taller than the width of the street in front of it plus twenty feet. This was done to ensure that no building was higher than the dome of the Capitol.

The Government Today

Today, Washington, D.C., bustles with activity. More than 300,000 people work for the federal government in Washington. That's more people than live in the entire city of Buffalo, New York!

The White House

The most famous government employee, of course, is the president. The president and first lady live at 1600 Pennsylvania Avenue. Their elegant home was not always called the White House. It was originally called the President's House. A short time later, newspapers started calling it the White House because of its walls (painted white to cover smoke damage from the War of 1812). But it wasn't until 1903 that President Theodore Roosevelt had the letterheads changed to White House.

Historic Tours of America c/o John Penney, Blackdog Advertising

George Washington is the only president who never lived in the White House. He died the year before it was finished, in 1799.

· · ·

When Theodore Roosevelt was in office, his lively children used the East Room for roller-skating.

· · ·

It takes 570 gallons of paint to cover the outside surface of the White House.

The **White House** is a lot bigger than it looks. It has 132 rooms, 35 bathrooms, 28 fireplaces, 8 staircases, and 3 elevators. For recreation, it has a tennis court, a jogging track, a swimming pool, a movie theater, and a bowling alley!

If you were able to get tickets in advance through a member of Congress, you'll get a twenty-five-minute tour of the most historic public White House rooms: the Green Room, Blue Room, Red Room, the State Dining Room, and the East Room—where the president holds press conferences and other large gatherings. In the East Room hangs a famous portrait of George Washington. First Lady Dolley Madison saved the painting during the War of 1812 when the British burned down the White House. It has been in the White House longer than anything else.

The fifty-four rooms upstairs are off-limits to visitors. They contain lots of storage areas and the living quarters of the president's family—about eight rooms. The Red, Green, and Blue rooms you see downstairs are used by the president only for entertaining guests.

Down the street from the White House is the Visitor's Center, which offers a continuously playing video tour. Here you can learn about the architecture and history of the White House, look at pictures of presidential families and pets, and read about interesting White House ceremonies.

White House Trivia

1. Who were the first occupants of the White House?
2. Who was the first and only president to get married in the White House?
3. What president was a major-league baseball broadcaster?
4. What president had pet silkworms and an alligator?
5. Who was the first president to ride in a car?

(Answers on page 147)

(Answers on page 147)

Did You Know?

Before 1975, vice presidents lived in their own private homes. Since then, vice presidents have lived in an official house right next to the National Naval Observatory on Massachusetts Avenue.

• • •

There have been seventeen weddings held at the White House. The most recent was in 1994 when then First Lady Hillary Rodham Clinton's brother, Anthony Rodham, married Nicole Boxer.

Fun Facts Crossword Puzzle

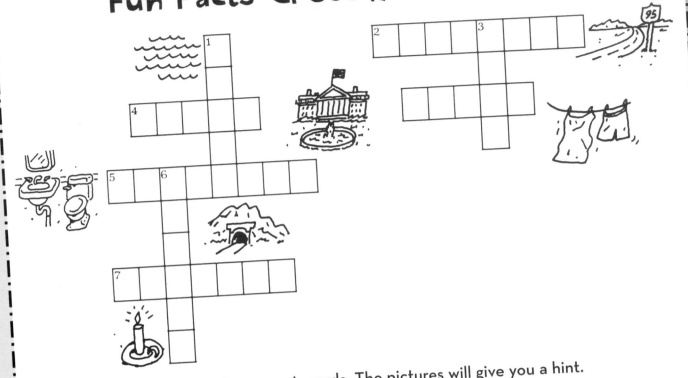

Fill in the blanks with the correct words. The pictures will give you a hint.

1. Running _ _ _ _ _ wasn't installed in the White House until 1834, when Andrew Jackson was president.

2. A "zero milestone," from which point all distances on U.S. _ _ _ _ _ _ _ _ are measured, is located on the ellipse just south of the White House.

3. John and Abigail Adams, the first residents of the White House, hung their _ _ _ _ out to dry in the East Room.

4. Thomas Jefferson competed in a national contest to design the _ _ _ _ _ _ _ _ _, but his plan was not chosen.

5. The first _ _ _ _ _ _ _ _ wasn't built in the White House until 1878.

6. It is possible to go in and out of the White House without being seen. There is a _ _ _ _ _ _ to the Treasury Department.

7. The White House was lit by _ _ _ _ _ _ _ until 1848, when gaslight was installed. Finally, electric lights were added in 1891.

(Answers on page 147)

The United States Capitol

The White House is the oldest public building in Washington, D.C., and the **U.S. Capitol** is the second oldest. It became the seat of government when lawmakers moved here from Philadelphia in 1800. Now, more than 8,000 new bills are proposed each year by senators and representatives.

Washington, DC Convention & Tourism Corp.

There are two senators from each state, regardless of its size. The number of representatives from each state depends on that state's population. For instance, Delaware has only one representative, while California has fifty-three. Senators and representatives meet in separate rooms, called *chambers,* in the Capitol. Together, these two legislative bodies are called *Congress.*

For daily free tours, you have to line up for passes first thing in the morning. Get in touch with your legislator well in advance of your visit if you want a VIP tour. You might even be able to meet your senator or representative in person. If you didn't call in advance, you can still drop by his or her office and see if there are passes to let you observe the Senate or House of Representatives in action. Ask someone to take you on the subway train that links the office buildings to the Capitol.

Did You Know?

The city that is the "seat of government" for a state or nation is called its *capital.* The building in which lawmakers meet is the *capitol.* The building where the lawmakers of the U.S. meet is called the *Capitol.*

You can look online or call to find out if Congress is in session. But why not use another method? Whenever the House or Senate is meeting, a flag flies over that chamber. And at night, a lantern on the roof is lit when either is in session.

The Capitol has a long history. Its most famous feature is the iron dome on top, which weighs nine million pounds and is the third largest in the world. The inside of the dome, or *rotunda,* is painted with scenes from American history. The artist painted someone's face (perhaps his own) in a tree trunk on one of the panels. Can you find it?

From the rotunda, on your way to the House of Representatives side of the Capitol, you will pass through Statuary Hall. This hall has statues of prominent people donated by each state. See if you can find your state's hero.

At one time, representatives met in this room. Ask a guide to demonstrate the mysterious echo the room makes. Find the plaque on the floor marking where John Quincy Adams suffered a

Did You Know?

VIP means *Very Important Person.*

• • •

The cast-iron dome of the Capitol will expand and contract as much as four inches on days of extreme temperatures.

Washington, DC Convention & Tourism Corp.

fatal stroke. Other plaques mark the seats of legislators—including Abraham Lincoln, who went on to become president.

Near the House chambers, climb the same stone spiral staircase British troops climbed when they set fire to the Capitol during the War of 1812.

Can you find the discoloration on the marble stairs leading to the White House Press Gallery? This was where, in 1890, a congressman was shot to death by a newspaper reporter during an argument about some articles the reporter had written.

Today the U.S. House of Representatives is the largest legislative chamber in the world. The leader, called the Speaker of the House, faces a semicircle of seats. There

Washington, DC Convention & Tourism Corp.

are no assigned seats, but Democrats always sit to the leader's right and Republicans to the leader's left.

Likewise, in the Senate, Democrats sit to the right and Republicans to the left of the vice president. But Senate seats are assigned.

Notice the saltshaker-like bottles on the desks of the hundred senators. They once contained pounce, which was used to blot ink. Many of the Senate desks date back to the early 1800s when the Capitol was rebuilt after being burned in the war. Some bear the initials of the legislators who sat in them. Jefferson Davis's desk has a patch on the side where a Union soldier struck it with a bayonet. Daniel Webster's desk does not have the extra writing box on top. And in every Congress since 1965 when Senator George Murphy started the practice, there has been a "Candy Desk" full of candy for senators to enjoy.

Boxes filled with snuff, a form of tobacco popular years ago, used to sit on ledges near the Senate speakers' platform. The boxes are still there, but the snuff is gone.

Do you see teenagers delivering messages in the two chambers? They are called *pages,* and you could become one. They attend a special school in the Library of Congress from 6:30 A.M. until about 10:30 A.M., then run to the Capitol to work while Congress is in session. To become a page, you need to apply and be chosen by your senator or representative. The competition is tough. Fewer than a hundred pages are chosen each year.

The U.S. Supreme Court

Until 1935 the **U.S. Supreme Court,** the highest court in the nation, met in the Capitol. It now has its own building across the street. You can't miss it. The building has sixteen columns of white Vermont marble three stories high and four bronze doors that together weigh twenty-six tons.

Test ⭐ Yourself

Q: Who was the first woman to sit on the Supreme Court?

A: Sandra Day O'Connor, who was appointed by President Reagan in 1981.

Did You Know?

Nine thousand cases are brought to the Supreme Court each term. But the justices select only one percent, or ninety, for consideration.

In most courts there is only one judge. But the Supreme Court has nine judges, called justices, who together decide cases. These justices are appointed by the president and approved by the Senate to serve in this job for life, or until they choose to retire.

From October through April, the court hears cases for two weeks at a time. It then switches to private meetings for the next two weeks. In May and June, the justices hear no new cases but meet to announce decisions.

The job of the Supreme Court justices is to apply the Constitution to new situations and decide if decisions made by lower courts, by Congress, and by the president are in keeping with the principles of the Constitution.

If you want to see the court in action, it's a good idea to arrive well before 10:00 A.M. since the chamber holds fewer than two hundred observers.

After the marshal opens the session, the justices, dressed in black robes, file in. The chief justice sits in the center. Notice the chairs, which are custom built to fit each justice. When a justice retires, the others buy the chair for him or her as a parting gift.

Tradition is very important in this court. White feather pens are still placed on the lawyers' tables every day, though no one uses them anymore.

On days when the court is not in session, every hour a guide gives a lecture on how the court operates. A movie on the ground floor runs whether court is in session or not.

The Library of Congress

The **Library of Congress** is next door to the Supreme Court. This is the official library for U.S. legislators. Each year library workers handle more than 500,000 inquiries from members of Congress and their staffs as well as from other branches of government. But that isn't their only task.

Another job is to assign library card catalog numbers to books. The library is also where all books, sheet music, film scripts, and other documents in America are copyrighted to protect them from being copied.

The Library of Congress is the largest library in the world. It has more than 130 million items, including books, magazines, photos, music, recordings, films, and maps. If the shelves were laid end to end, they would stretch from Washington, D.C., to Detroit, Michigan.

The Great Hall through which you enter is breathtaking with its fancy dome, statues, murals, inlaid floor, carvings, and columns. When the first of the three buildings, the Thomas Jefferson Building, was completed in 1897, it was described as the "most beautiful building in the world."

Many historic documents are preserved here, including Thomas Jefferson's rough draft of the Declaration of Independence, letters written by George Washington, and Abraham Lincoln's Gettysburg Address, as well as the contents of his pockets on the night he died. There are diaries and notebooks kept by Alexander Graham Bell, who invented the telephone; magic scrapbooks of Houdini; and personal papers of comedian Groucho Marx and other famous people.

There's also a collection of 2,100 early baseball cards from 1887 to 1914. These cards were originally distributed in cigarette packs. Legendary figures and events such as Ty Cobb stealing third base for Detroit, Tris Speaker batting for Boston, and pitcher Cy Young are included.

The library's smallest book is *Old King Cole*. It measures $1/25$-inch x $1/25$-inch, or about the size of the period at the end of this sentence. You need a needle to turn the pages! And you've probably heard of Stradivarius violins—the finest in the world. Well, the Library of Congress has one of these, too. These valuable items are not on display, but people doing research can study them.

One priceless item that is on exhibit is an original copy of the Gutenberg Bible, the first book ever printed in movable type.

The National Archives

You can see the original Declaration of Independence, as well as the Bill of Rights and the Constitution. They're in the **National Archives**. These documents are so old the ink is faded. The glass that protects them has filters and is filled with a special gas that keeps light and air out to prevent the documents from fading further.

The National Archives is sometimes called the *national memory* because it houses all of the nation's official paperwork. Here papers are sorted and decisions are made to store or destroy them. Patents, census and immigration records, pension files, photographs, treaties, motion pictures, and other documents dating as far back as 1775 can be found here.

The National Archives is also famous for genealogical research. (*Genealogy* is the study of family trees.) Here you can trace your family back to discover where your ancestors were from and who you are related to. You may be surprised to find some important historical figures in your family!

Historic Tours of America c/o John Penney, Blackdog Advertising

Famous Documents

Do you know what the missing words are to the famous lines of these historical documents?

Declaration of Independence (second paragraph)

We hold these truths to be self-evident, that all _ _ _ are created _ _ _ _ _, that they are endowed by their Creator with certain unalienable _ _ _ _ _ _, that among these are Life, _ _ _ _ _ _ _, and the pursuit of Happiness.

Constitution (preamble)

We the People of the _ _ _ _ _ _ _ _ _ _ _ _, in Order to form a more perfect Union, establish _ _ _ _ _ _ _, insure domestic Tranquility, provide for the common defense, promote the general _ _ _ _ _ _ _, and secure the Blessings of Liberty to ourselves and our Posterity, do ordain and establish this Constitution for the United States of _ _ _ _ _ _ _.

Bill of Rights (the First Amendment of the Constitution)

Congress shall make no law respecting an establishment of _ _ _ _ _ _ _ _, or prohibiting the free exercise thereof; or abridging the freedom of _ _ _ _ _ _, or of the _ _ _ _ _; or the right of the people peaceably to assemble, and to petition the Government for a redress of grievances.

(Answers on page 147)

The Bureau of Engraving and Printing

This is where the money is—tons and tons of it. Every day, at the Washington **Bureau of Engraving and Printing** and at a second printing facility in Fort Worth, Texas, thirty-three million notes are manufactured, totaling $529 million. Approximately 2,500 people work around the clock in three shifts, five days a week. Notice the security guards and cameras watching you.

Most of the money made is used to replace worn-out bills. The $1, $5, and $10 bills are printed most often. The $20 bills are printed less often, and $50 and $100 bills are only printed occasionally. Bills of larger sizes—$500, $1,000, $5,000, and $10,000—have not been printed since 1969 because there are already enough.

Bureau of Engraving and Printing

Did You Know?

Contrary to popular belief, the car pictured on the back of the $10 note is not a Model T Ford. It is just a creation of the man who designed the bill.

• • •

Every year the Bureau of Engraving uses 4.8 million pounds of "paper" and $14 million worth of ink.

• • •

If the U.S. Treasurer stays in office for five years, his or her signature will be on 5.8 billion dollar bills.

47

Did You Know?

No trees have been cut down to make these bills. They are not actually made of paper. They are made of cloth—75 percent cotton and 25 percent linen.

Test Yourself

Q: What is the life expectancy of a $1 bill?

A: With normal usage, a $5 bill lasts twenty-two months. A $5 bill lasts two years; a $10 bill lasts eighteen months; and a $100 bill will be around for five years.

Q: Why is there no demand for $500 or $1,000 bills nowadays?

A: With checks and credit cards available, people have no need to carry such large sums of money.

Through a series of windows you can watch the bills being made. Large sheets of special "paper" are pressed under engraved steel plates coated with security ink. On one day, the green ink side of the bills is printed and on the next, the black ink side. Each large sheet contains thirty-two bills. Watch as the printed sheets roll off the press in stacks of ten thousand. Each stack of $1 bills is worth $320,000. The sheets are then cut apart and each bill is inspected for defects. Making a $1 bill takes three to five days from start to finish.

Starting in 2003, the U.S. government issued bills ($10, $20, $50) with new safety features to foil counterfeiters. The most noticeable difference is the use of orange, yellow, and red background colors. These colors are embedded in the paper when the paper is produced. When the paper arrives at the Bureau of Engraving and Printing, these bills are printed with the same green and black ink used on the other bills.

Near the gift shop, you can see the Bureau of Engraving and Printing's display of a $100,000 bill (the highest denomination ever printed) and money no longer in use. Don't be disappointed that coins are not made here. That's the job of the Bureaus of the Mint in Philadelphia and Denver.

Think about this: If you had ten billion $1 notes and spent one every second of every day, it would take you 317 years to go broke. Wow!

The Bureau of Engraving and Printing doesn't just print money. Postage stamps are printed here, as well as identification badges, treasury bonds, and even White House invitations.

Pretend that you're the president and design the invitation below for a special party. And since you're the president, you can also design your very own postage stamp.

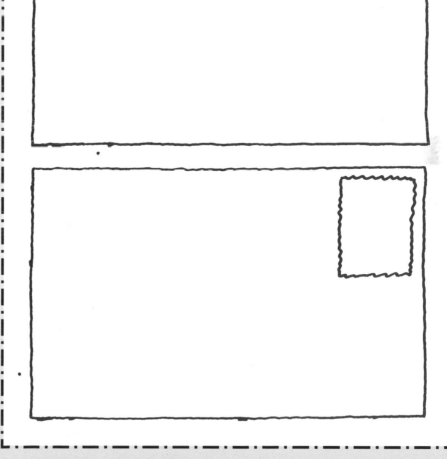

Glimpses of the Famous

When you think of Washington, D.C., you can't help but think of George Washington, Thomas Jefferson, Abraham Lincoln, Franklin Delano Roosevelt, John F. Kennedy, Martin Luther King Jr., and other famous leaders. Your visit will give you a chance to learn more about the lives of these and other great individuals.

George Washington

Other than the name of the capital itself, the most famous memorial to George Washington is the **Washington Monument,** which looks to some people

Courtesy of the Mount Vernon Ladies' Association

like a giant pencil. It towers 555 feet over the Mall and is the world's tallest masonry structure. At its base, the marble walls are fifteen feet thick. There is nothing holding the stones together but gravity. The monument was planned in 1783, but Washington never got to see this majestic tower. Building didn't start until 1848, nearly fifty years after the first president's death, and it wasn't completed until 1884. If you look closely, you'll notice the color of the marble changes about 150 feet from the base of the monument. This was the height of the tower when work stopped for twenty-two years before and during the Civil War. When building resumed, the marble came from another level of the quarry.

If you want to go up in the Washington Monument, you can get advance tickets from the National Park Service website. The other option is to go to the kiosk on 15th Street first thing in the morning. There are a whopping 897 steps to the top, but visitors aren't allowed to walk up them. They have to take the elevator instead. The ride takes seventy seconds—a far shorter time than the original steam elevator ride that lasted twenty minutes. The view from the top is perhaps the best in all of Washington, D.C. The Capitol is to the east, the White House to the north, the Jefferson Memorial to the south, and the Lincoln Memorial to the west.

Washington, DC Convention & Tourism Corp.

Park rangers lead special "walk down" tours so you can see the 192 memorial stones donated by individuals, societies, states, and nations. Tour times vary depending on the day and the season, so ask a park ranger for details.

To get a sense of George Washington as a person, you should visit **Mount Vernon,** George and Martha Washington's home, only sixteen miles south of D.C. in Virginia. The house is filled with eighteenth-century treasures. Around the estate you'll see beautifully restored buildings such as a greenhouse, stables, slave quarters, and a kitchen. And at the museum you'll get a firsthand look at the first president's false teeth. They're not made out of wood as is commonly believed but out of a mix of human teeth, cow's teeth, and elephant tusk.

Courtesy of the Mount Vernon Ladies' Association

Thomas Jefferson

The **Jefferson Memorial,** honoring the third president, Thomas Jefferson, is another must-see in Washington. Its columns and domes echo the style Jefferson used to design his own home, Monticello, and the rotunda at the University of Virginia. The interior of the dome bears famous writings of Jefferson, who was one of the authors of the Declaration of Independence. A nineteen-foot, five-ton bronze statue of this great champion of religious and racial freedom stands in the center. Check out the exhibit that highlights Jefferson's life and watch the ten-minute video. If you have questions, National Park Service employees are always there to answer them. The most thrilling time to visit is in the evening, when the Jefferson Memorial is brightly lit.

"I am as happy nowhere else, and in no other society, and all my wishes end, where I hope my days will end, at Monticello." Thomas Jefferson did indeed die at **Monticello,** which includes a house, extensive gardens, and a large plantation near Charlottesville, Virginia, about two hours outside of Washington, D.C. Here you can take a guided tour of his extraordinary home and grounds, and see how Jefferson and his family lived in the late 1700s.

New York Historical Society, New York City

Did You Know?

Thomas Jefferson, with no formal training, designed Monticello himself. He also founded the University of Virginia.

Historic Tours of America c/o John Penney, Blackdog Advertising

Did You Know?

Coincidentally, a few weeks before he shot President Lincoln, John Wilkes Booth rented the same room in the Peterson House and slept in the same bed where Lincoln later died.

Abraham Lincoln

You can see the gun that killed President Lincoln, bone fragments from his skull, and the room in which he died on April 15, 1865.

Start at **Ford's Theatre,** where actor John Wilkes Booth shot President Lincoln. See the box seat where Lincoln sat that fateful night, then go downstairs to where the **Lincoln Museum** has the clothing he wore when he was shot, a blood-stained pillow, and Booth's gun and riding boot (slit down the side because he broke his leg during his escape). Read Booth's own diary explaining why he killed Lincoln, whom he blamed for the Civil War: "I can never repent it, although we hated to kill. Our country owed all her trouble to him [Lincoln], and God simply made me the instrument of his punishment."

Across the street is the **Peterson House,** often called the "House Where Lincoln Died." To see skull fragments and the bullet that killed Lincoln, you need to go to the **National Museum of Health and Medicine** in the Walter Reed Army Medical Center. This unusual museum also has a collection of microscopes, early X-ray equipment, and preserved body parts, including the amputated leg of Civil War general Daniel Sickles. In addition, you can see live leeches and a human hair ball that was extracted from a six-year-old girl's stomach.

National Park Service

There is another place honoring President Lincoln that you won't want to miss—the **Lincoln Memorial**. It's at the west end of the long, narrow reflecting pool that runs to the Washington Monument. It has thirty-six marble columns, one for each state in the Union at the time Lincoln died.

Inside, Lincoln sits larger than life. Lincoln was six feet four inches tall, but this statue is nineteen feet high and weighs one hundred and fifty tons. Engraved in the walls are Lincoln's famous Gettysburg Address and his second inaugural address. Take a look on the steps for the engraving marking the spot where, in 1963, Martin Luther King Jr. made his famous "I have a dream" speech.

Franklin Delano Roosevelt

Unlike the Lincoln and Jefferson Memorials, which are focused on a single, covered statue, the **Franklin Delano Roosevelt Memorial,** completed in 1997, has four outdoor "rooms," one for each of FDR's terms in office. (Until 1951, a president was allowed to serve more than two terms in office.) The memorial has beautiful shade trees, waterfalls, statues, and granite walls with quotes, which together tell the story of Roosevelt as president through the Depression years and World War II.

Look for familiar quotes such as "The only thing we have to fear is fear itself" and for the sculpture of Roosevelt's beloved dog, Fala. In the fourth room you'll see a sculpture of Eleanor Roosevelt, the first time a first lady has been honored in a presidential memorial.

Terry J. Adams, National Park Service

John F. Kennedy

There is a living memorial to a more recent president. The **John F. Kennedy Center for the Performing Arts,** opened in 1971, is a national cultural center. There are seven different theaters in this gigantic center: the Concert Hall, the Opera House, the Eisenhower Theater, the Family Theater, the Terrace Theater, the Theater Lab, and the Jazz Club. These theaters offer a range of performances by the best musical, theater, and dance groups in the world.

Even if you don't go to a performance, there's plenty to see. Take a free fifty-minute tour or explore on your own. (There are interactive video displays in the halls on John Kennedy as well as information on the current presentations.) Make sure you visit the Hall of Nations,

Did You Know?

The Washington Monument could be placed on its side in the Grand Foyer and still have seventy-five feet to spare!

• • •

Italy donated the 3,700 tons of marble used in the Kennedy Center building.

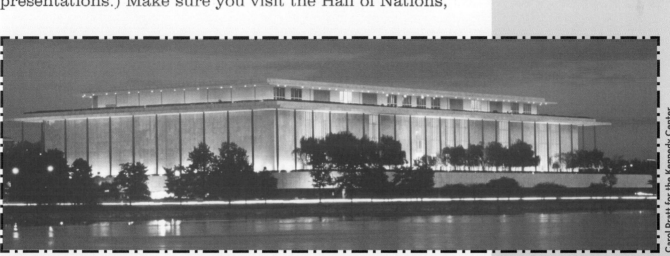

where all the flags of countries recognized by the United States are displayed in alphabetical order, and the Hall of States, which is lined with the flags of the fifty states, five territories, and the District of Columbia. In the red-carpeted Grand Foyer you can see a seven-foot bronze bust of John F. Kennedy. Many countries gave incredible gifts to the center in memory of Kennedy, such as the crystal chandeliers from Sweden and Austria, the gold silk stage curtains from Japan, the beautiful tapestries from different African countries, and a 4,500-year-old alabaster vase from Egypt.

If you want to go to a show, you have many choices. The regular programs include symphonies, operas, plays, dance performances, music concerts (from jazz to pop), and tribute ceremonies. There are also special performances geared to families (and some, such as the daily performances at the Millennium Stage, are free). Call for details.

Martin Luther King Jr.

Between the Lincoln and Jefferson Memorials is the **Martin Luther King Jr. National Memorial**. To honor this great American civil rights leader, the memorial's designer chose to use the natural elements of water, stone, and trees to highlight the themes of justice, democracy, and hope that Dr. King so eloquently spoke

Did You Know?

Dr. Martin Luther King Jr. is the first African American to receive his own memorial on the Mall—and only the third nonpresident to be honored in this way.

about. A thirty-foot likeness of Dr. King will be integrated into the centerpiece of the memorial, called the "Stone of Hope," from his "I have a dream" speech. The memorial also includes inscriptions of quotes from this famous civil rights activist's sermons and speeches.

Many Great Americans— Known and Unknown

John F. Kennedy and close to 290,000 other U.S. heroes are honored nearby in the most famous cemetery in the country—**Arlington National Cemetery**. It is in Virginia, just across the Potomac River from the Lincoln Memorial.

A flame burns constantly at Kennedy's grave. Once, on a visit to the former mansion of Civil War general Robert E. Lee, which overlooks the cemetery, President Kennedy was overheard remarking about the peaceful feeling he had. "I could stay here forever," he said. Kennedy's wife and two of their children who died very young are buried nearby, but not John F. Kennedy Jr., whose ashes were scattered over the Atlantic Ocean where he died in a plane crash in 1999. Near President Kennedy's grave is the grave of his brother, Senator Robert Kennedy, who was also assassinated.

At this cemetery you'll find the graves of other famous people as well: President William Howard Taft; Pierre L'Enfant, the first city planner of Washington; Abner

Did You Know?
Three of the first five presidents died on July 4: Thomas Jefferson, John Adams, and James Monroe.

Doubleday, the founder of baseball; boxer Joe Louis; Virgil Grissom, Edward White, and Roger Chaffee, the three astronauts killed in a 1967 test spacecraft explosion; Supreme Court justices Oliver Wendell Holmes, Earl Warren, Thurgood Marshall, and William Rehnquist; Audie Murphy, the most decorated hero of World War II; and astronauts Mike Smith and Dick Scobee, who died in the 1986 explosion of the *Challenger.*

Perhaps the most moving monuments of all are those for the less famous men and women who have given their lives for this country. While in Arlington National Cemetery, stop at the **Tomb of the Unknowns,** dedicated to those killed in World Wars I and II and the Korean and Vietnam wars but whose bodies could not be identified.

Historic Tours of America c/o John Penney, Blackdog Advertising

Soldiers from the Army's 3rd U.S. Infantry (The Old Guard) guard the tomb year round. Carrying an M-14 rifle, these volunteer "sentinels" march twenty-one steps, click their heels, turn to face the tomb for twenty-one seconds, then turn back and repeat the process. Every half hour during the summer and every hour the rest of the year, there is a changing of the guard ceremony.

Just north of the cemetery is the **Marine Corps War Memorial**—a statue showing marines raising the U.S. flag at Iwo Jima during World War II. It's the biggest statue made from a single piece of metal in the world.

Back on the Washington, D.C., side of the Potomac, near the Lincoln Memorial, is the **National World War II Memorial,** opened in 2004 to honor the sixteen million people who served in the U.S. Armed Forces during the war and the more than 400,000 who died. Look for your state inscribed on one of the fifty-six pillars arranged in a semicircle around a pool and fountain. Two arches representing the Atlantic and the Pacific stand on opposite sides. The big wall to the west of the memorial is called the Freedom Wall. Each of the 4,048 gold stars represents one hundred people who died in the war.

Not far from the Capitol is the **National Japanese American Memorial**. A stunning sculpture of two cranes holding barbed wire, struggling to break free, is the center of this memorial to honor the 30,000 Japanese Americans who served in the U.S. military during World War II, and to commemorate the 120,000 men and women who were put in ten internment camps. There is also a memorial wall made of pink granite, a pool containing several large boulders, and a memorial bell to recall the tradition of Japanese temple bells.

One of the most visited sites in Washington is the **Vietnam Veterans Memorial,** a V-shaped marble wall bearing the 58,253 names of those who were killed in the war or are still missing in action. Veterans' names appear in order of the date they died. Near "The Wall," you'll find two statues. One is *The Three Soldiers,* which shows three servicemen who seem to be looking at the wall. The other is the *Vietnam Women's Memorial,* showing two women caring for a wounded soldier while another looks on.

On the other side of the reflecting pool is the **Korean War Veterans Memorial,** dedicated in July of 1995. This memorial depicts nineteen larger-than-life sculptures representing brave infantrymen dressed in battle gear. The inscription reads, "Our nation honors her sons and daughters who answered the call to defend a country they never knew and a people they never met."

The historic U Street neighborhood is the home of the **African American Civil War Memorial**. The sculpture features uniformed black soldiers and a sailor getting ready to leave home, in honor of the African American troops who fought in the Civil War. At the **African American Civil War Memorial Museum,** just two blocks away, you will see a variety of news articles and objects from this period, including an 1834 bill of sale for a young girl in Alabama.

There's one more memorial you may want to check out. Dedicated by President George W. Bush in 2005, **The Extra Mile—Points of Light Volunteer Pathway** honors Americans who, through caring and personal sacrifice, built their dreams into great movements that have created change in America. Honorees (twenty so far) include Cesar Chavez, Helen Keller, Harriet Tubman, and Booker T. Washington. Each one has a custom-made bronze medallion installed along the sidewalk just blocks from the White House. Eventually there will be a total of seventy, forming a mile-long pathway beginning at the corner of 15th Street and Pennsylvania Avenue, across from the U.S. Department of the Treasury.

Did You Know?

The average age of the men who fought in World War II was twenty-six. The average age in Vietnam was twenty-three.

• • •

Close to ten thousand women served in Vietnam, mostly as nurses. Eight of these died.

Can You Name These Monuments?

1. _____

4. _____

2. _____

5. _____

3. _____

6. _____

(Answers on page 147)

The Mall and Mr. Smithson

Washington has some of the greatest museums in the world. And it's all thanks to a man who never even visited America.

James Smithson was an Englishman dedicated to learning. In 1829 he willed the U.S. government $500,000 to be used to expand knowledge. As a result, the Smithsonian Institution was founded. A number of the Smithsonian's museums line the Mall and can be visited on the same day.

The Castle

This was the first Smithsonian building and is easily recognizable for its turrets and dark red (sandstone) color. **The Castle** opens one and a half hours earlier (8:30 A.M.) than the other Smithsonian buildings, so head to the Information Center here to learn about special events and to map out your museum visits.

Historic Tours of America c/o John Penney, Blackdog Advertising

National Museum of American History

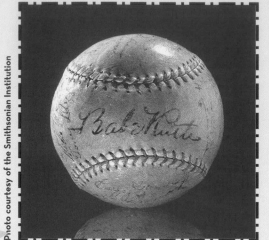

The original Star-Spangled Banner, the flag that flew over Fort McHenry in Baltimore during the British attack in the War of 1812, can be seen at the **National Museum of American History**. In fact, this museum is chock full of Americana.

You will also see Ben Franklin's walking stick, the microphone Franklin D. Roosevelt used for radio broadcasts, and Abe Lincoln's hat.

You'll learn about inventions that changed the way Americans live: Thomas Edison's electric lightbulb and first record player, Eli Whitney's cotton gin, Henry Ford's Model T car, a real 280-ton steam engine, and an atom smasher.

You're sure to get a kick out of the display of gowns worn by first ladies through the years. Notice how small some of the women were 150 years ago!

One of the museum's highlights is the exhibit of items from American pop culture. Check out the ruby slippers Judy Garland wore in *The Wizard of Oz,* jazz king Dizzy Gillespie's trumpet, the boxing gloves of Muhammad Ali and Joe Louis, and Kermit the Frog. You can see Julia Child's kitchen, Mr. Rogers's sweater, and Fonzie's jacket.

An exhibit called The Price of Freedom: Americans at War surveys the history of America's military. You'll learn about the impact of war on soldiers, their families, and their communities and see objects such as George Washington's sword, the buckskin coat worn by George Custer in 1875, and a restored UH-1H Huey helicopter from the Vietnam era. You'll also find General Colin Powell's uniform from Operation Desert Storm.

In the America on the Move exhibit you'll get the chance to see a 1903 Winton, the first car driven across the United States, a Chicago "L" train car, and a forty-foot piece of the famous Route 66.

In addition to these exhibits, the National Museum of American History will offer many new things to see when it reopens in 2008 after renovations.

Did You Know?

The earliest evidence of life is 3,500 million years old. To see it, look in the Earliest Traces of Life Gallery.

Photo courtesy of the Smithsonian Institution

National Museum of Natural History

As you enter the **National Museum of Natural History** you'll meet a gigantic, twelve-ton African bush elephant (stuffed, of course). It is the largest elephant ever taken from Africa.

In the Kenneth Behring Family Hall of Mammals you will find close to three hundred stuffed animals from all over the world. The eleven-foot-long Bengal tiger is believed to be the largest ever killed in India. You will learn about how mammals evolved by adapting to changing habitats. Look for "Morgie," one of the Earth's first mammals, who lived during the time of the dinosaurs, 210 million years ago.

Dinosaur Hall is a treasure house of fossils and prehistoric bones. You can't miss the replica of the

Photo courtesy of the Smithsonian Institution

Tyrannosaurus rex or the *Triceratops*. How long is his horn? If you're interested in a huge dinosaur footprint, a dinosaur egg that's seventy million years old, or a plant-eating dinosaur called a *Diplodocus* that was eighty foot long and weighed twenty-five tons, this is the place for you.

Next, see if you can find the fossil of a $2^1/2$-foot camel-like animal that used to live, believe it or not, in Nebraska.

If you're squeamish, you may not want to go into the Orkin Insect Zoo. This exhibit is full of enough living, creepy-crawly creatures to last a lifetime—gigantic cockroaches, centipedes, tarantulas, beetles, leaf-cutting ants, huge grasshoppers, and hermit crabs, to mention just a few. There are working anthills and beehives, too. And don't miss the prehistoric dragonfly—it has a five-foot wingspan!

A highlight of the Museum of Natural History is the Janet Annenberg Hooker Hall of Geology, Gems, and Minerals. Any fortune-teller would be jealous that the world's largest crystal ball, more than twelve inches in diameter and 106 pounds, is here. A more recent acquisition is an extremely rare 23.1-carat Burmese ruby. How about wearing a necklace the size of the Hope Diamond? It's 45.5 carats and the largest blue diamond in the world.

The diamond necklace that French emperor Napoleon gave to his wife, Marie Louise, is in this exhibit, as is her crown with 950 diamonds, and the earrings worn by French queen Marie Antoinette before she was beheaded during the French Revolution.

Don't leave without a trip through the colorful Crystal Gallery, where you will learn everything you need to know about crystals. Take a walk through a re-created copper mine and see how minerals and ores are formed, mined, and used in our society.

Want to touch a meteorite or a piece of Mars? If so, head to the Earth, Moon, and Meteorite Gallery. Or if you are interested in creating an earthquake, you'll get your chance in the Plate Tectonics Gallery.

Try timing your visit when the first-floor Discovery Room is open. (Call in advance for specific dates and times.) This room features hands-on exhibits and games. Handle mastodon teeth, a crocodile head, fossils, a stuffed porcupine, a snakeskin, coral, and bones. Examine minerals under microscopes. Play drums from Kenya or dress in foreign costumes.

If you need a break from walking around, you could take in a film about wildlife, geography, or natural history at the museum's IMAX theater.

Washington, DC Convention & Tourism Corp.

National Gallery of Art

Next to the Museum of Natural History across 7th Street is the **National Gallery of Art**. This museum is actually two buildings. The focus in the East Building is modern art. A giant Alexander Calder mobile dominates the atrium as you enter. You'll also find works by Pablo Picasso, Henri Matisse, and Joan Miró.

Take the "people mover" on the lower level to get to the West Building, which has art dating back to the Middle Ages (thirteenth century). The West Building has the only Leonardo da Vinci painting in the Western Hemisphere, artwork by famous Old Masters like Rembrandt and Rubens, and works by French, Spanish, and American artists. Some of the gallery's most exciting works include

Rubens's painting of Daniel in the lion's den; Titian's portrait of a twelve-year-old boy, painted 450 years ago; August Renoir's picture of a girl with a watering can; and Winslow Homer's painting of a fisherman with three boys.

If you want more detailed information on a specific work of art, go to the Micro Gallery near the rotunda, where you can use touch-screen monitors to look up artist biographies, specifics of cultural and historical events related to individual works of art, or definitions of art terms in an illustrated dictionary.

The Sculpture Garden, opened in 1999, has a reflecting pool and fountain. There's one sculpture here you can touch—*Six-Part Seating* by Scott Burton—but the others are worth seeing as well. In winter, the pool and fountain are converted to an ice-skating rink open to the public.

If you have time, look outside at the acute angle of the southwest corner wall of the East Building. So many people have touched it, the stone has been polished smooth.

Did You Know?

It isn't by chance that the West Building's dome looks like the dome of the Jefferson Memorial. The two buildings were designed by the same man: John Russell Pope.

. . .

A Lady Writing, the painting by Johannes Vermeer referenced in the novel, *Chasing Vermeer*, by Blue Balliett, is hanging in the West Building of the National Gallery of Art.

National Museum of the American Indian

The **National Museum of the American Indian,** opened in 2004, is the first national museum dedicated exclusively to Native Americans. All the exhibits are presented from the Native American viewpoint.

Notice the outside walls. Made of limestone, they give the feeling of being weathered by wind and water for thousands of years. Close to three-quarters of the museum site is the outdoor landscape, which has four sections: meadow, crops, woods, and wetlands. Medicinal plants fill the crop area, as well as corn, beans, squash, and tobacco. More than twenty-five species of trees help to shade the museum site. Forty boulders, known as "grandfather rocks," represent Native peoples' ancestors.

The entrance to the museum was purposely placed facing east toward the rising sun. Once you're inside, see how beautifully the light reflects off the prism window. The atrium is called the "Potomac," a Piscataway word meaning "where the goods are brought in," and is meant to honor Native peoples from the Washington, D.C., area.

Can you recognize any of the words on the screen above the Welcome Desk? This is the Welcome Wall, with the spoken and written words in Native languages from all over the Americas.

In the Our Universes exhibit, you can see a twinkling star canopy above the gallery and watch an animated story about stars. Window on Collections features a variety of handmade dolls, a walrus head made of motorcycle parts, and a toy buffalo made from real buffalo hide.

Besides the exhibits, there is an excellent thirteen-minute presentation on the fourth level called *Who We Are*. This multimedia experience explains the diversity of today's Native American Indians.

If you're hungry, you can visit one of the most popular of the museum restaurants here. At **Mitsitam** you can see salmon being smoked over an indoor fire pit and sample Native American dishes such as an Indian taco made with fry bread.

Before you leave, stop by the Resource Center and use one of the computer stations to learn more about Native cultures. Then send an e-postcard to someone back home.

Photo by Ernest Amoroso, NMAI

Did You Know?

Early native tribes such as the Aztecs, Incas, and Mayans used gold to make sculptures, masks, and other ceremonial objects. With the arrival of the Europeans came the practice of using gold to make coins.

. . .

In 1819, a Cherokee man named Sequoyah was the first to write the Cherokee language, called a *syllabary*. Within three years, most Cherokees learned to write using this syllabary. Both written and spoken Cherokee are still widely used today.

. . .

Mitsitam means "let's eat" in the language of the Delaware and Piscataway Indians.

National Air and Space Museum

The story of aviation is best told at the **National Air and Space Museum**. This is the most visited museum in the world, probably because in one spot you can see everything from the actual 1903 *Flyer* used by Orville Wright to fly over Kitty Hawk, to the command module of *Apollo 11,* which landed on the moon.

You can walk under airplanes, satellites, rockets, and spacecraft that hang from the ceiling. You can walk in and around others.

Of special interest are Charles Lindbergh's *Spirit of St. Louis*; the *Skylab* Orbital Workshop, which shows how people live in space; John Glenn's Mercury capsule *Friendship 7,* which made America's first manned flight around the earth; the X-15, the fastest plane ever built; and *SpaceShipOne,* the first privately developed, piloted vehicle to reach space.

You can also see a pedal-powered airplane; the plane in which Amelia Earhart flew solo across the Atlantic in 1932; a U-2 spy plane; and a replica of the Soviet's *Sputnik,* the first satellite in orbit.

The How Things Fly gallery on the first floor has more than fifty interactive exhibits. You can watch wind-tunnel demonstrations and sit in a Cessna 150 cockpit.

And don't miss touching the four-billion-year-old moon rock. It's near the Mall entrance to the building.

You can climb inside a flight simulator and experience the thrill that pilots feel, or go to the Lockheed Martin IMAX theater showing, among other things, *To Fly!* The Albert Einstein Planetarium has a twenty-minute tour of the universe called *Infinity Express.* Tickets go fast, so buy them on arrival.

Can you name the planets in our solar system? Their names have been scrambled to give you some hints.

CRUMEYR _____

NSEVU _____

HEART _____

RAMS _____

RIPEJTU _____

RUNSTA _____

SUNUAR _____

PEENUTN _____

(Answers are on page 148)

77

Photo courtesy of the Smithsonian

Hirshhorn Museum and Sculpture Garden

There's a very unusual sculpture plaza outside the drum-shaped **Hirshhorn Museum**. You'll find it behind the building on Jefferson Drive. Let's see how skilled you are in a sculpture hunt.

In the garden and on the outdoor plaza of the museum, see if you can find the following: the *Geometric Mouse* made of black aluminum; a statue of a singing girl, called *Song*; and a rabbit as *The Drummer*. Can you find *The Three Red Lines*? (Hint: They're thirty-seven feet tall and sway in the wind.)

Locating Kenneth Snelson's *Needle Tower* is hardly like finding a "needle in a haystack." The tower is as high as a six-story building. Look under the "needle" for a star. See it?

Be sure to find *The Burghers of Calais* by French sculptor Auguste Rodin. (Burghers, pronounced like *hamburgers* without the *ham*, are townspeople; and Calais is a seaport in France.) Look carefully at the eyes of the men.

Inside the building, pick up a Family Guide at the Information Desk. With this series of sturdy, colorful cards you can look for specific works, learn something about them, and tell stories about what you see. This museum is full of treasures such as the sculpture *Bus Riders*, by George Segal. Can you figure out how the artist made the people look so real? He wrapped fabric soaked in plaster on real people, much like doctors do to make a cast.

For his mobile, *Fish*, Alexander Calder used buttons, pieces of colored glass, and pieces of pottery to look like shiny scales. And don't miss famous American painter Jackson Pollock's *Number 3, 1949: Tiger*. Instead of using paintbrushes, Pollack used a stick to dip and splash the paint on a canvas on the floor.

Did You Know?

Africa is the second largest continent in the world and is home to around one thousand different ethnic groups who speak as many languages.

• • •

Because African tribes moved around a lot, they carried their valuables with them or wore them as jewelry. The size of a woman's gold earrings was a sign of wealth. The bigger the earrings, the richer she was.

National Museum of African Art

A unique collection of art of a different kind is only steps away in the **National Museum of African Art,** which boasts a collection of artwork from all parts of the African continent.

Notice the nearly life-size beaded carving of a German soldier who befriended an African king. There are also bronze portraits of Nigerian kings, traditional African costumes, musical instruments, and jewelry. Imagine wearing the huge gold earrings that are often supported by a leather strap! See if you can find the bird carved into an ivory spoon, the wooden headrest that is shaped like an elephant, or the pipe carved into a train.

Freer Gallery of Art and Arthur M. Sackler Gallery

Together, the **Freer Gallery of Art and Arthur M. Sackler Gallery** house one of the world's finest collections of Asian works. Chinese jades, bronzes, and paintings, Japanese screens, early biblical manuscripts, and miniatures from India and Persia are exhibited here.

Charles Lang Freer (1854–1919) bequeathed his extensive collection of Asian art to the Smithsonian. The gallery opened in 1923. Freer was introduced to Asian art by the American artist James McNeill Whistler, whose work was influenced by Japanese art. In London in the late 1800s, Whistler was hired by Frederick Leyland to repaint the shutters and doors of his dining room. Whistler ended up painting the whole room blue and gold, with peacocks adorning the walls. Leyland, not happy with what Whistler had done, only agreed to pay half of Whistler's fee. Whistler, to retaliate, painted a mural on the south wall with two peacocks in an aggressive stance. At one bird's feet are silver coins. These represent the money Leyland refused to pay. Whistler called this mural *Art or Money; or, the Story of the Room*. Years later, the dining room was dismantled and Charles Freer bought Whistler's creation and had it moved from London in 1904 to his home in Michigan. Today it's one of the highlights of the Freer Gallery.

Did You Know?

In 1993, to celebrate the reopening of the Peacock Room after extensive restoration, the Freer Gallery brought Henry, a peacock, and Sylvia, a peahen, to live in the museum courtyard. Sylvia was laying too many eggs, so after a year, the birds were given to a farmer.

Courtesy of the Freer Gallery of Art and Arthur M. Sackler Gallery

United States Holocaust Memorial Museum

Opened in April 1993, the **United States Holocaust Memorial Museum** includes a large permanent exhibit called The Holocaust and a smaller one called Remember the Children: Daniel's Story.

The Hall of Witness at the U.S. Holocaust Memorial Museum. Photo by Alan Gilbert, courtesy USHMM, Photo Archives

No entry pass is needed for Remember the Children: Daniel's Story. In this interactive exhibit you follow Daniel and his family as they struggle to survive persecution by the Nazis. Daniel and his father survive, but his sister and mother do not. At the end of the exhibit there's a place for you to draw a picture or write your thoughts about what you saw.

You need to get a same-day timed entry pass to get into The Holocaust exhibit. The average visit is two to three hours. Be prepared for lots of reading during this self-guided tour where you track the progress of World War II from Hitler's rise to power through the liberation of the camps after Germany was defeated. Interspersed in the exhibit are artifacts, photos, film, and eyewitness testimonies from a variety of people during the period between 1933 and 1945 when six million Jews were systematically persecuted and murdered. Gypsies, Poles, people with disabilities, and many others also suffered under Nazi tyranny.

At the end of the exhibit, you'll see the Hall of Remembrance, the nation's memorial to the victims of the Holocaust.

Front view of the railcar on display at the U.S. Holocaust Memorial Museum
Photo by Edward Owen, courtesy USHMM, Photo Archives

Beyond the Mall

In the old days, you could see almost everything Washington had to offer by traveling up and down the Mall. Not anymore. Now there are museums, galleries, and monuments all over D.C. Luckily, some new favorites are clustered in an area of downtown about a mile northeast of the White House.

International Spy Museum

Courtesy of the International Spy Museum

There are more spies in Washington than in any other city in the world. So you're in the right place to see this amazing collection of spy tools, including an American CIA (Central Intelligence Agency) disguise kit, a Russian spy coat with a buttonhole camera, and a pistol in a lipstick container.

Start your visit to the **International Spy Museum** by selecting a "cover." As a spy you choose a new identity and a "legend," the story that supports your identity. Remember to stop at the marked checkpoints as you make your way through the museum, to make sure you are keeping your cover.

The School for Spies exhibit describes the skills essential to being a spy, as well as how spies are recruited and trained. Test your ability to identify someone in disguise.

Courtesy of the International Spy Museum

See how it feels to crawl through an air duct so you can listen to a private conversation in the room below.

You'll learn how long spying has been around when you see the life-sized masked Ninja representing the art of invisibility in twelfth-century Japan. In the United States, George Washington was the first politician to use spying to gather information. But spying only became a formal part of the U.S. government in the early days of the Soviet Union.

World War I marked the first use of cameras for spying. Spies studied photos to learn about enemy weapons and to make maps. Often, pigeons outfitted with tiny cameras were released over military sites. While the birds flew, the cameras clicked away, snapping pictures that were developed and studied when the pigeons returned to their owners.

Courtesy of the International Spy Museum

Are you good at cracking codes? Learn about the Enigma code machine used by the Germans during World War II.

In the War of the Spies exhibit you'll hear spy catchers tell stories of how they caught real modern-day spies like Aldrich Ames and John Walker.

Before you leave the museum, you can find your home on Google Earth. And remember to stop for a debriefing session to see if you successfully kept your cover.

Right next door to the museum is **Spy City Cafe,** where you can sneak a bite to eat. Choose from a Langley Dog, a Red Square Dog, a Disguise Dog, and an All-American Dog. Sandwiches and salads are also available.

Smithsonian American Art Museum and the National Portrait Gallery

Ken Rahaim, Smithsonian Institution

These two museums are housed in one of the oldest buildings in Washington, D.C., completed in 1868.

Highlights of the **Smithsonian American Art Museum** are the craft and modern folk art collections. One favorite is *Bottlecap Giraffe,* a giraffe made from bottlecaps; another is a massive throne made mostly of gold and silver aluminum foil called *Throne of the Third Heaven of the Nations Millennium General Assembly.* James Hampton, a janitor working at the General Services Administration, spent more than ten years building this structure made of wood, glass, and plastic material, and covered in gold and silver foil. The throne was found in a garage in 1964, after the artist's death.

In the third floor's contemporary art exhibit you'll find a map of the United States made from more than three hundred TVs. Artist Nam June Paik created this work so that if you stand in the right spot, you can see yourself in Washington, D.C.! And check out David Hockney's *Snails Space with Vari-Lites, Painting as Performance.* Have a seat and watch as the colored lights change in sequence.

The **National Portrait Gallery** features portraits of the presidents, including a famous one of George Washington by Gilbert Stuart. This same artwork is on the $1 bill. If time allows, stop by the Lunder Conservation Center, where you have the unique opportunity to watch conservators through floor-to-ceiling glass walls repairing damaged works and preserving new acquisitions.

National Building Museum

This is an awesome structure made of fifteen million bricks! Originally built to be a modern office building for the Pension Bureau, today the **National Building Museum** is a museum about the art and science of building.

Before you enter the museum, take a minute to look up at the terra cotta frieze encircling the building. It shows a parade of Civil War military units in a pattern repeated every seventy feet.

The museum inside is fifteen stories high and is as long as a football field. Stop at the information desk for a copy of the "Adventures in Architecture Scavenger Hunt." See if you can meet the challenge to identify, sketch, and analyze a variety of architectural features around the building.

Make sure you visit the permanent exhibit, Washington: Symbol and City, where you can touch models of some of Washington's most famous buildings or play interactive question-and-answer games on architecture. If you have young siblings, you might want to take them to the second floor Building Zone, where they can build a brick wall, drive a bulldozer, or dress up with a hard hat, tool belt, and goggles.

National Postal Museum

The **National Postal Museum,** across the street from Union Station, offers you the chance to experience what it's like to drive a mail truck, ride in a stagecoach, or work in a railway post office train car. Look at the creative mailboxes from rural America and see a stuffed version of "Owney," the Postal Service's unofficial mascot at the end of the nineteenth century. Owney, a stray dog who started riding with mail bags on railway service trains across the country, was considered a good-luck charm because no train he ever rode was in a wreck.

If you like interactive exhibits, you can chart the route a letter might take or address a postcard and watch it find its destination. And definitely visit What's in the Mail for You? where you'll learn how companies use information to

Did You Know?

The eight big columns inside the museum are made of bricks—70,000 each!

Did You Know?

The ZIP in ZIP code stands for Zoning Improvement Plan. ZIP codes were started on July 1, 1963.

• • •

The rarest U.S. postage stamp, the "One-Cent Z Grill," was issued in 1868 and is a portrait of Benjamin Franklin. Market value: $3,000,000.

sell you their products through the mail. You get to make your own ID card, with your picture and individual information (true or made up). Then you learn how companies compile this information and use computers to create a letter personalized just for you.

National Museum of Women in the Arts

Today, learning about how caterpillars turn into butterflies is fun, but imagine being the first person to document the process, step by step. Maria Sybilla Merian, a German artist who lived from 1647 to 1717, was also a scientist. She was fascinated by moths, butterflies, and other insects from the time she was a child. Merian raised the insects and drew them live, rather than drawing them after they were dead, as was the practice during that time. In addition to being beautiful, her work was revolutionary in its scientific accuracy. The **National Museum of Women in the Arts** features a number of Merian's drawings of butterflies, bugs, and plants.

Other works by women in this collection include *The Bath* by American artist Mary Cassatt. This print reflects the popularity of Japanese art among Western artists during the 1890s. Take a look at *Alligator Pears in a Basket,* an early drawing by Georgia O'Keeffe. Do you know what we call this fruit today? Avocados.

The Corcoran Gallery of Art

The **Corcoran Gallery of Art** is known for its collection of American art, including work by portrait artists John Singleton Copley, Gilbert Stuart, and Rembrandt Peale. Look at Peale's portrait, *George Washington Before Yorkshire*. Washington's horse in the picture, named Nelson, was really brown not white (although Washington did have some white horses).

You'll also find the thirteenth-century stained-glass window from France's Soissons Cathedral and a painting by Aaron Douglas, *Into Bondage,* of African people being taken as slaves from their native land.

Frederick Douglass National Historic Site

Start at the visitor's center of the **Frederick Douglass National Historic Site,** where you can see a bronze statue of Douglass and pictures of his family. To get the story on Douglass's life, watch the film, *Fighter for Freedom: The Frederick Douglass Story*. You'll learn that Douglass never knew his parents. His mother was a slave and his father was a white man. Douglass was sold as a slave when he was eight and was secretly taught to read by his owner's wife.

Test Yourself

Q: Can you find Frederic Edwin Church's 1857 painting of one of the Seven Wonders of the World? Which one is it?

A: Niagara Falls.

Douglass went on to become an active abolitionist. A brilliant speaker, he traveled extensively, giving lectures on the need for voting rights and other civil liberties for African Americans. Park rangers will take you through Douglass's last home, Cedar Hill, where you can get a good feel for how Frederick Douglass lived.

Did You Know?

Women were not allowed to vote in U.S. federal elections until 1920, when the Nineteenth Amendment to the U.S. Constitution was passed.

Sewall-Belmont House and Museum

The **Sewall-Belmont House and Museum** on Capitol Hill is dedicated to preserving a crucial piece of history—the fight for the American woman's right to vote. This struggle is documented in a significant collection focused on suffrage and equal rights movements. Some of the art and artifacts in the museum tell the story of Alice Paul, who founded the National Woman's Party and dedicated her life to getting equal rights for women.

The National Air and Space Museum's Steven F. Udvar-Hazy Center

This companion museum to the Air and Space Museum on the Mall is in a humongous hangar next to Dulles International Airport, which allows plenty of space to fit more than 125 aircraft and 140 spacecrafts.

Two highlights of the **National Air and Space Museum's Steven F. Udvar-Hazy Center** are the Boeing 367-80, the first commercial jet in the United States, and the world's fastest aircraft, known as the *Blackbird.* You can also see the Concorde, which flew at 1,350 miles (2,173 km) per hour—twice the speed of sound. Make sure to take the time to visit the observation tower, where you can get a nice view of airplanes at Dulles Airport taking off and landing.

Photo by Carolyn Russo/NASM, National Air and Space Musem, Smithsonian Institution

If you're into space, you can see a prototype of the space shuttle *Enterprise,* the world's first and only reusable space

vehicle. Test vehicles for the Mars *Pathfinder* and *Sojourner* are also here. On July 4, 1997, *Pathfinder* landed on Mars. The equipment operated through solar panels that opened up after landing. Then, *Pathfinder* rolled off to take pictures and collect data on rocks and soil. The mission lasted three months.

Photo by Dane Penland, National Air and Space Musem, Smithsonian Institution

What Else Is There?

There's a lot more to this city than museums and galleries. There are beautiful gardens, canal boats to ride, games to play, and places so old it's like traveling back through time.

A Town Within a City—Georgetown

Georgetown is a charming part of Northwest Washington, brimming with history. It was the first port on the Potomac River. Ships unloaded luxury goods and furniture from England in exchange for tobacco from the colonies, bringing London elegance to this small port city. Many of Georgetown's brick "row houses" are one to two centuries old. The oldest house in Washington (built in 1765) is on M Street, and looks very much like it did before the American Revolution. You can visit the **Old Stone House,** where people who are dressed in colonial garb demonstrate some homemaking tasks such as spinning and quilting.

Washington, DC Convention & Tourism Corp.

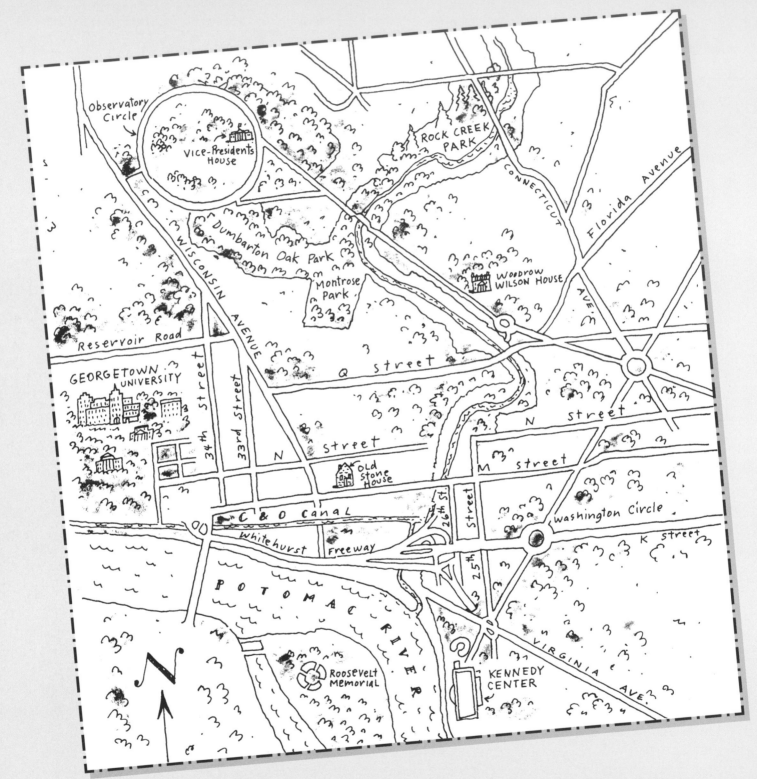

One block south of the Old Stone House runs the **C&O Canal,** where mule-drawn boats were once used to haul cargo. The boats still operate on the Chesapeake and Ohio Canal from April to October, but carry tourists instead of cargo. Today, people often jog and bike along the mule "towpath."

NPS photo by Terry Adams

At the north end of Georgetown is **Dumbarton Oaks,** a beautiful old estate with a museum, terraces, fountains, and gardens perfect for romping.

Next to Dumbarton Oaks is **Oak Hill Cemetery,** with many old tombstones. Look over by the chapel for the grave of John Howard Paine, author of the song "Home, Sweet Home."

Another cemetery of note is the **Mount Zion Cemetery,** at 27th and Q Streets, which was established in 1842 and provided burials for freed slaves.

Did You Know?

The Chesapeake and Ohio Canal was designed to link Washington, D.C., to Pittsburgh, Pennsylvania, in the 1820s. It was only finished as far as Cumberland, Maryland. Railroads turned out to be faster.

• • •

A canal boat could carry as much as 120 tons of coal from the mountains of Maryland to the port of Georgetown. A family lived aboard the canal boat and the children walked alongside the mules on the towpath to make sure the mules behaved.

• • •

During World War II a conference held at Dumbarton Oaks laid the groundwork for the creation of the United Nations.

• • •

At 2803 P Street you'll find a fence made of Civil War musket barrels.

Did You Know?

You can find the "Exorcist Steps" (ninety-seven of them) leading from Prospect Street to M Street in Georgetown. These steps were used in the filming of the movie *The Exorcist* in 1973.

• • •

Francis Scott Key, author of "The Star-Spangled Banner," used to live at 3512 M Street, NW, in Georgetown. A freeway is there now, but a bridge that connects Georgetown to Virginia bears his name.

• • •

Many of the sites referenced in Anne Spencer Lindbergh's *The People in Pineapple Place* are real places in Georgetown.

Walking or riding along the cobblestone streets of Georgetown is fun. Take a look at the houses where famous people once lived: John F. Kennedy stayed at 3307 N Street before he was president; Jackie Kennedy lived at 3017 N Street after her husband was killed; Robert Todd Lincoln, the only surviving son of Abe Lincoln, lived at 3014 N Street. Elizabeth Taylor lived at 3252 S Street when she was married to Senator John Warner.

The only former president's house in Washington open to the public is the **Woodrow Wilson House** at 2340 S Street, just east of Georgetown. Wilson lived in this house after he left the White House until his death in 1924. The house is just as it was then. You can see objects from the White House and elaborate gifts of state from around the world. The house is also a living textbook of "modern" American life in the 1920s, from sound recordings to silent films to flapper dresses still hanging in the closets. Also of interest are the elevator built in 1915 and the kitchen, which has a coal stove and oven and one of the first electric refrigerators.

As you walk around Georgetown, do you notice all the college students? They most likely attend **Georgetown University,** the nation's oldest Catholic and Jesuit university. What started in 1789 as a small group of students and teachers has grown into a major international university including undergraduate and graduate programs, a law school, and a medical school.

Something Old, Something New

This place looks old but is actually quite new. Here are a few clues to its identity. Can you guess what it is?

It's where President Woodrow Wilson and Helen Keller are buried, but it is not a cemetery.

Its foundation stone contains a rock from a field in Bethlehem and was laid by a U.S. president.

Martin Luther King Jr. preached his last sermon here.

Historic Tours of America c/o John Perney, Blackdog Advertising

You're right: It's a church. But not just any church. It's the **Washington National Cathedral,** a modern version of a fourteenth-century Gothic cathedral. Creating a national church was a dream of George Washington, but work on the cathedral wasn't actually begun until 1907.

Like the ancient cathedrals, it has flying buttresses, gargoyles, and stained-glass windows. A reminder that the cathedral is modern, however, is the piece of moon rock embedded in the stained-glass "Space Window." See if you can find it. Then see if you can locate the Lincoln pennies in the floor.

Did You Know?

Services have been held in the Washington Cathedral daily since 1912.

• • •

A flying buttress is a stone arch coming out from a wall to support it. There is no structural steel in the Washington Cathedral.

• • •

Gargoyles, which look like devilish creatures, are used as waterspouts. They carry water away from a building through a hole in their mouths.

Q: Which country has been the chief trading partner of the United States?

A: Canada.

Q: When it is summer in the United States, which season is it in Australia?

A: Winter.

Q: To which city would you fly to visit the Vatican, walk through an ancient forum, and tour the Baths of Caracalla?

A: Rome.

Q: Which state borders the most Canadian provinces?

A: Montana.

Science and You

You're probably familiar with *National Geographic* magazine. It takes readers on pictorial trips to the far corners of the globe and galaxy. Imagine walking into the pages of the magazine and you've just pictured the **National Geographic Museum at Explorers Hall,** where you can investigate the Earth's deserts, jungles, mountains, oceans, and even outer space through various temporary exhibits, photos, and films.

On permanent display are three-dimensional models of the Grand Canyon and Mount Everest as well as state-of-the-art relief maps and artifacts.

You can take a long walk or hop the Metro to get to the **Albert Einstein Memorial,** tucked into a grove on the grounds of the National Academy of Sciences (the NAS is a society of scholars doing scientific research—there's nothing to see in the building). Einstein, a brilliant physicist who lived from 1879 to 1955, is portrayed sitting and holding some pages. Written on these papers are the three equations Einstein is most famous for

coming up with: the photoelectric effect, the theory of relativity, and the equivalence of energy and matter ($E=mc^2$). Feel free to sit on Einstein's lap and see if some of that brain power rubs off!

Military Matters

The **Pentagon,** headquarters of the U.S. military, is located across the Potomac River in Virginia. It is the world's largest office building—25,000 people work here! Imagine 17.5 miles of hallways, 280 bathrooms, and 150 staircases in one building! Aside from the five-sided structure itself, though, there is not a lot to see—except offices! The Pentagon is not open for tours to the public.

Did You Know?

The employees of the Pentagon make 200,000 phone calls and send 1,000,000 e-mails daily.

Did You Know?

Cannons on board nineteenth-century frigates such as the *Constitution* weighed three tons and needed nine to fourteen men to load and shoot them.

• • •

The DSV (Deep Submergence Vessel), *Trieste*, went to the deepest part of the ocean to see if anything could live at 35,000 feet below sea level. Yes, it found sea life.

Near the Pentagon, look up to see three curved steel spires soaring more than two hundred feet into the air. The **U.S. Air Force Memorial,** opened in 2006, honors the service and sacrifices of the men and women of the U.S. Air Force.

If you're excited by military things, far more interesting is a stop at the Navy Yard in southeast Washington. This used to be where weapons were made, but now it's the **U.S. Navy Museum**. You can aim the barrel of a World

War II ship's gun, turn submarine periscopes, operate anti-aircraft weapons, and go aboard a destroyer. Try deciphering messages at the Battle of Midway computer game.

Be sure to ask about the museum's scavenger hunt, which sends you searching for various weapons and military gear. There are guns and ship models dating from Revolutionary War times to today, including a ship model that used to be in President Kennedy's office.

What's Wrong with This Picture?

There are 10 things in the Navy Yard that shouldn't be here. Can you find them?

(Answers on page 148)

The Great Outdoors

If you're looking for an extended break from being inside, there are lots of options for outdoor fun.

East Potomac Park is a 1$\frac{1}{2}$-mile stretch of land in southwest Washington. There's a path for walking, a playground, and—for warmer weather—an outdoor pool, tennis, and miniature golf. There are also two 18-hole golf courses.

In Georgetown you'll find **Montrose Park,** which has tennis courts, picnic tables, a playground, and lots of open space for games.

If you prefer to get out of the city, **Candy Cane City** (or Meadowbrook Park) in Chevy Chase, Maryland, offers a variety of playground equipment with soft elasticrete for cushioning your feet! It also has ball fields, tennis courts, and a picnic area.

Hadley's Playground in Potomac, Maryland, is a one-acre fully accessible playground for kids with disabilities. This park offers a creative play course that is perfect for skates, bikes, and wheelchairs.

Wheaton Regional Park and **Cabin John Park,** also in Maryland, offer year-round ice-skating in addition to ball fields, tennis courts, playgrounds, and hiking trails.

Like to climb rocks? If so, then head to **Great Falls,** a waterfall and park next to the Potomac River in Potomac,

Maryland. (You can also see the falls from Great Falls, Virginia.) You can't swim here, but you can climb, fish, or go kayaking. Take the restricted area signs seriously; the current is very strong and dangerous. If you prefer to just stand and watch the wild water, a walk to Olmstead Island will give you a great view.

Stopping to Smell the Roses

Where can you see seventy thousand azaleas, a dye garden, and a tree more than three centuries old? How about a type of redwood tree that grew when dinosaurs walked the earth twenty-five to forty million years ago?

If you guessed the **United States National Arboretum**, a 446-acre garden in northeast Washington, D.C., you were right. This amazing garden also has dwarf evergreen trees and miniature bonsai trees. Special gardens grow herbs from which medicines were made, herbs used for cooking, and herbs used to dye clothes.

There are 9.5 miles of road to travel down and numerous footpaths to wander along. If you don't feel like walking, take the 35-minute tour on the tram. Don't miss the reflecting pool containing colorful Japanese koi that look like giant red goldfish. The most exciting time to visit is in the spring, when the azaleas, dogwoods, cherry blossoms, and wildflowers are in bloom.

Did You Know?

Bonsai trees never get big because they are clipped constantly. The arboretum has one that is more than 360 years old but will only reach your knees.

. . .

Willow was the original source of aspirin. You'll find it in the arboretum's herb garden.

Color in the flowers and trees and unscramble their names.
The pictures will give you hints.

GOODWOD _ _ _ _ _ _ _

ALEASZA _ _ _ _ _ _ _

MORECHOSRYSSBL _ _ _ _ _ _ _ _ _ _ _ _ _ _

CHORDSI _ _ _ _ _ _ _

PRAYSUNFELTV _ _ _ _ _ _ _ _ _ _ _

ROBENASIET _ _ _ _ _ _ _ _ _

LATESILEWIR _ _ _ _ _ _ _ _ _ _

(Answers on page 148)

If it's impossible for you to get to the arboretum, try to see the **United States Botanic Gardens** on the Mall at the foot of the Capitol. The highlight of this giant greenhouse is orchids—there are always about 250 on display. And there are plenty of other flowers, all in a lush, relaxing setting of waterfalls, pools, and fountains. See the vanilla orchid, which gives us vanilla flavoring; the chocolate (cacao) tree, whose seed is used to make chocolate; and the coffee tree, which produces coffee beans. During the summer months you can see plants that eat insects, such as the Venus flytrap.

For a different kind of garden, try **Kenilworth Park and Aquatic Gardens** in northeast Washington, which has a huge number of water lilies and aquatic plants. This floating garden has been described as a treasure hidden away from Washington's mainstream. See lotus blossoms as big as a human face and water lilies that are red, blue, pink, and purple. In August, you can see a lily that has leaves measuring five feet in diameter. This garden also has about forty ponds linked by trails, and untold numbers of frogs, turtles, birds, muskrats, and raccoons.

Where Are All the Animals?

The National Zoological Park

Washington isn't just a city of historical figures, diplomats, and politicians. There are other famous residents—of the four-legged variety. For instance, you can see Kandula, the young Asian elephant who weighed 335 pounds when he was born at the zoo in 2001, and Komodo dragons, the largest living lizards, reaching lengths of more than ten feet and weighing over 300 pounds.

Jessie Cohen, Smithsonian's National Zoo

These creatures and many others can be found at the **National Zoological Park,** located in Rock Creek Park. The best time to visit is in the early morning or the late afternoon, when the animals are most active.

The first thing to do when you arrive at the zoo is to stop by the Visitor Center for a map and a list of programs being offered that day.

The giant pandas from China and their baby, Tai Shan, are among the most famous residents of the zoo. You'll find them, along with a number of other animals, in the Asia

Image courtesy of the Smithsonian's National Zoological Park

Trail exhibit. Since pandas spend around sixteen hours a day eating, you might see them chewing away on bamboo, which makes up 99 percent of their diet. Each panda can eat up to forty pounds of bamboo a day!

In addition to the pandas, try to visit the Reptile Discovery Center and the cheetahs—the fastest land animals in the world.

The Amazonia exhibit re-creates the Amazon River and rain forest. On the ground floor you can see many colorful river fish. Upstairs are monkeys and birds moving freely through the exhibit.

Make sure you visit the invertebrates (creatures that don't have backbones). And don't leave without stopping by the Great Ape House to watch the antics of the gorillas and orangutans. You can follow them as they travel outside on towers and cables to the Think Tank, a research center

Did You Know?

Smokey the Bear may look brown, but he is really an American black bear.

• • •

Giraffe tongues can be as long as twenty-one inches.

Test Yourself

Q: Do you know what it means to be *extinct*?

A: *Extinct means that every member of an animal or plant species has died. Tyrannosaurus rex, dodo birds, and woolly mammoths are all extinct species.*

Q: Do you know what it means to be *endangered*?

A: *Endangered means that a species is in danger of becoming extinct. Very few of that species are left or the population is quickly diminishing. The zoo's giant pandas, cheetahs, and orangutans are all endangered.*

Did You Know?

There are around 2,400 animals from four hundred species at the National Zoo. About 20 percent of these species are endangered.

where orangutans communicate with biologists through touch-screen computers.

One way to get close to the animals is through the walk-in Flight Cage where you can mingle with one hundred different kinds of birds.

The National Zoo even has a Kid's Farm, where you can see and pet all your favorite farm animals. You can also play on a huge toy pizza while you learn about how the ingredients for pizza are grown.

More Zoos

There are two smaller zoos in the area, one in Virginia and one in Maryland. Among the animals you'll see at the **Reston Zoo** in Reston, Virginia, are zebras, antelope, and bison—and you don't have to walk. Take the Zoofari wagon tour and rest your feet.

At the **Catoctin Wildlife Preserve and Zoo** in Thurmont, Maryland, you'll find ostriches, swans, tigers, and a jaguar. During the summer months you can even ride a camel! Both zoos close during the winter, so be sure to check dates and hours of operation before you go.

Test Yourself

Q: What is the fastest land mammal?

A: Cheetahs—that can run up to 70 MPH.

Q: What is the fastest flying bird?

A: Peregrine falcons—that can dive toward the earth at more than 200 MPH.

Q: What is the fastest fish?

A: Sailfish—that can swim up to 68 MPH.

Q: What is the deadliest animal to humans?

A: Female Anopheles mosquitoes that, by carrying malaria, kill more than one million people each year.

Q: What is the strongest animal?

A: The rhinoceros beetle, which can lift 850 times its own weight.

A creature from outer space got into the zoo and zapped the animals with its vanishing gun. Fortunately, the gun didn't work correctly and parts of the animals can still be seen. Help restore the animals by adding the correct letters to the names below.

Hint: They have lined up in alphabetical order.

AN_EL_PE
BA_OON
CHE_TAH
DE_R
E_LEPH_NT
_OX
G_RAF_E
YEN
I_UANA
JAG_AR
KAN_A_OO
LE_PARD
M_USE

_IGHTINGA_E
O_L
P__DA
_UAIL
RA__OON
SQ_IR_EL
TI_E_
_NICO_N
VAM_IRE BA_
WO_F
X
YA_
ZE_RA

(Answers on page 149)

Did You Know?

Zombies are people who have been put in a trancelike state in order to obey the commands of others. Sometimes they are called *the walking dead.*

The National Aquarium

There are more than 250 species and 1,700 underwater creatures waiting to entertain you at the **National Aquarium,** located in the basement of the Department of Commerce building in downtown D.C. This museum is small, but there's plenty to see.

One interesting species you'll see at the aquarium is the puffer fish. Can you find one? Did you know that medicine men in Haiti used the poison found in these fish to create zombies?

Or perhaps you'd like to watch the piranhas at dinnertime. They're the flesh-eating fish that swim in schools of thousands. If you're visiting during feeding time you're not allowed to crowd around the tank, tap on the glass, or bother the fish in any way. It makes them nervous and then they won't eat.

Other attractions are a seven-thousand-gallon tank full of sharks, live sea horses, and two alligators named Crunchy and Munchy.

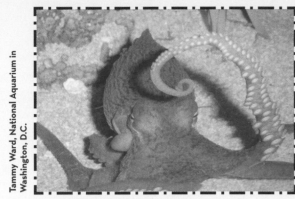

Tammy Ward, National Aquarium in Washington, D.C.

And then there's Shania, the giant Pacific octopus from Canada. See if she's playing with one of her many toys. Shania has shown talent at opening bottles, unlocking hamster balls, and taking the pieces off toys such as Mr. Potato Head to find food hidden inside.

Unusual Farms

There are lots of other fun places to see animals in and around Washington, D.C. There are many farms, but not the kind of farms you're used to. One farm operates just like it did in colonial times. Another lets you help bring in the harvest, milk a cow, or cook a meal. Still another has animals roaming free. Be careful not to step on a chicken!

The **Claude Moore Colonial Farm at Turkey Run** in McLean, Virginia, is the farm of a lower-income family living in 1771. A family in costume goes about the daily chores using only eighteenth-century tools and planting only eighteenth-century crops. They may even invite you to help with the chores!

Photo by Marcia Christian of Claude Moore Colonial Farm

Did You Know?

Children on a colonial farm learned farming skills from the time they were toddlers by working alongside their parents in the fields.

• • •

Storytelling was a primary form of entertainment, much as television is today.

At the **National Colonial Farm** in Accokeek, Maryland, you'll see a middle-class tobacco plantation from 1775. Don't be surprised to find chickens and turkeys running free (the hogs, sheep, and cattle are in pens). In those days, crops were fenced in for protection, while the animals roamed at will.

Believe it or not, you can see a stuffed two-headed calf in the veterinarian's office of the **Carroll County Farm Museum** in Westminster, Maryland. This mid- to late-1800s farm has a farmhouse, blacksmith and tinsmith shops, nature trails, and a collection of horse-drawn vehicles to be explored. Baby goats, lambs, pigs, turkeys, chickens, and rabbits can be seen in the barns during the warmer seasons.

If you want to help gather eggs, milk a cow, or grind feed for the horses, head to a working farm from the 1900s called **Oxon Hill Farm** in Oxon Hill, Maryland.

For Nature Lovers

You'll find **Rock Creek Park Nature Center** located in the midst of 1,750 acres of hardwood forest, the last remaining forest within Washington, D.C.'s city limits. The exhibit hall has an owl, snakes, toads, turtles, and a working beehive. Test your senses on the Touch Wall, where you stick your hand in a hole and guess what you're feeling. Nearby, you can catch the center's planetarium show.

Outside the city in Maryland are two other nature centers. The first, **Brookside Nature Center** in Wheaton, Maryland, has live animal exhibits and a fascinating butterfly exhibit in the spring. You might be lucky enough to have a butterfly land right on you!

Second is the **Croydon Creek Nature Center** in Rockville, Maryland, where you can see a rare albino corn snake; "Rover," an Eastern box turtle who's missing part of his top shell (it was eaten by a dog); and Homer, a black rat snake. Challenge yourself on the geo-safari computer game or become a high-tech birder through the computer program Maryland Birds.

The **Patuxent National Wildlife Visitor Center** opened in 1994, but the refuge surrounding it was established by Franklin Delano Roosevelt in 1936. Learn all about our environment through hands-on exhibits; travel through life-size habitat areas; peer into the worlds of endangered species; and observe wildlife for yourself through binoculars and telescopes.

Did You Know?

Black rat snakes are Maryland's largest snake species. They grow on average between six and eight feet long, but they are not venomous.

• • •

Box turtles live an average of eighty years.

• • •

One of the ongoing projects at the Patuxent Wildlife Research Center is to repopulate the wild with whooping cranes. The number of these endangered birds reached an all-time low in 1941, when there were only twenty-one birds left in the wild. Today, thanks to the efforts of a number of groups, babies are being raised in captivity and then released, resulting in a wild flock of 194 birds.

What's the Score?

Be it basketball, hockey, baseball, soccer, or football, Washington, D.C., has a professional sports team for you.

Conveniently located in downtown D.C., the **Verizon Center** is home to the NBA's Wizards, the WNBA's Mystics, and the NHL's Capitals. If you call in advance and aren't too picky about where you sit, you have a good chance of seeing one of these teams in action.

Washington, DC Convention & Tourism Corp.

The **Washington Wizards,** originally the Chicago Packers in the early '60s, then the Baltimore Bullets, and later the Washington Bullets, became Washington's basketball team in 1997. The years since 1997 have been up and down for the Wizards, but they're still a team worth watching. Washington fans are hoping that one day they'll be able to repeat the incredible 1977–78 season played by their earlier incarnation, the Washington Bullets. Their season runs from early November until late April.

Another option is to cheer on the **Mystics,** Washington's WNBA team. This team started play in 1998, the second year of the WNBA. If you have a favorite player, you can high-five her as she enters the court. Just stand outside section 109/110 before the game starts. The WNBA season starts when the NBA season is ending in May. The women play through the summer until mid-August.

If you're visiting Washington during the winter and are a hockey fan, you're in luck. You can see the Caps—the **Washington Capitals**—who have been in Washington since 1974. So far they haven't won a Stanley Cup, but they have made it to the play-offs many times. When you're at the game, take a break to check out the Hockey 101 booth, where you can ask questions, learn fun facts, and maybe even shake "hands" with the team mascot, Slapshot, the eagle.

If you prefer baseball, go see the **Washington Nationals**. Nicknamed the "Nats," this team played in Montreal as the Expos before they came to Washington for the 2005 season. This is not the first baseball team for the nation's capital. Between 1901 and 1961 two other teams called Washington home. Still, it had been almost fifty years since the city had had its own team, so when the Expos were looking to move from Montreal, Washington, D.C., lobbied hard, and won.

Test Yourself

Q: Which high-profile basketball player joined the Wizards team for two seasons in 2001–2003?

A: Michael Jordan.

Q: Which football team lost to the Washington Redskins in their first game in Washington in September 1937?

A: The New York Giants.

As for soccer, the world's most popular sport is gaining popularity in the United States, too. Washington's **D.C. United** was one of the original teams in 1996 when the United States started a professional league called Major League Soccer. The D.C. team's record has been impressive. They've won the MLS championship four times: in 1996, 1997, 1999, and in 2004, so if you're in town during soccer season (April to October), head to RFK Stadium to watch D.C. play.

"Hail to the Redskins!/Hail Victory!/Braves on the warpath!/Fight for old D.C.!" This is the chorus for the NFL's **Washington Redskins** fight song, sung faithfully by Redskins fans, especially at their hometown FedEx Field in Landover, Maryland. Even though they haven't won a Super Bowl since 1991, this team has many die-hard fans. Unfortunately, you won't get regular-priced tickets to a Washington Redskins game because they're all sold to season ticket holders.

But all hope isn't lost. If you're in D.C. on a fall Sunday and have to watch football, head to the **ESPN Zone** sports bar, restaurant, and family fun center. It's just a few blocks from the Verizon Center downtown. Upstairs you can watch sports on giant-screen TVs, and downstairs you can play a variety of games with sports themes.

Can I Have That?

You'll probably have trouble choosing among the variety of original gifts and unusual souvenirs in Washington, D.C. For instance, you can wow your friends back home by serving astronaut freeze-dried ice cream or giving them a lollipop with a real scorpion in it. How about showing your classmates your invisible journal or some colonial currency? Teach your neighbors a ball-and-cup game played by colonial children, or let them feel your genuine fossilized shark's tooth.

All these souvenirs and many more can be had in the shops of Washington's museums. These places specialize in items that are affordable, popular, and often impossible to find anywhere else.

Did You Know?

Two-dollar bills have not been printed since 1976 because they aren't very popular. But they are still around. You can buy them at the Bureau of Engraving and Printing's gift shop.

Your Own Museum Collection

The National Air and Space Museum offers astronaut freeze-dried ice cream in four flavors; laser pointers that light up the wall with different images; Mars Mud, a bouncy, stretchy play dough; and some really cool gyroscopes.

The Bureau of Engraving and Printing will sell you newly printed money, or for a lower price, bags of shredded bills.

The National Aquarium not only has fossilized sharks' teeth but some great models of lizards and turtles. Or how about a stuffed-animal jellyfish?

And speaking of stuffed "animals," when you're visiting the National Museum of Health and Medicine, you could add a cough or cold stuffed "germ" to your collection.

At the National Colonial Farm you'll find colonial-style toys, such as a wooden ball-and-cup toss, tops, and tin whistles.

Whole packets of fake colonial or revolutionary wartime currency are for sale at the Ford's Theatre Book Shop. Or if you're a fan of Thomas Jefferson, when you're at his memorial, you'll find quill pens not unlike the one Jefferson himself used.

At the National Archives Building, you can pick up copies of our nation's Declaration of Independence, Constitution, and Bill of Rights.

Feel like you need to get people's attention? Head to the Supreme Court gift shop, where you can buy a mini gavel or one that doubles as a pencil!

If fossils or gemstones are more your style, stop in at the Museum of Natural History gift shop, where fake fossils, colorful necklaces, and bracelets are both attractive and affordable. Also stock up on amber candies with mealworms in them and the scorpion lollipops.

For gadget lovers, the International Spy Museum store offers a spy voice trap. Record your message, set the alarm, and hide! When your intruder arrives, they trip your alarm and hear your message. You can also get a journal that you can write in with invisible ink.

For an extra-special gift, how about a flag that has flown over the Capitol? You can get one, only they have to be ordered through your senator or representative. Allow four to six weeks for delivery.

Did You Know?
The Pavilion tower has ten large bells just like those in England's Westminster Abbey.

Markets, Malls, and Stalls

Museum shopping is fun and easy because you're already there. But Washington also has plenty of malls and shopping areas that are worth a visit.

To get a local flavor for Capitol Hill, go to the **Eastern Market,** the last of Washington's nineteenth-century markets still in operation. In addition to all sorts of fresh foods, there is a flea market and an arts-and-crafts fair. This is a perfect shopping destination during warm weather.

Another fun place to shop is the **Old Post Office**. This 1899 building was converted into a treasure chest of about sixty stores, craft outlets, and an international eatery called the Pavilion. You'll recognize the building by its 315-foot clock tower. Inside, ride the glass elevator to the top for a stunning city view. Afterward, browse among the shops. Check the schedule for music and other entertainment.

A mall with some very unusual stores right downtown is the **Shops at National Place**. Above its three levels of shopping and fast-food outlets, rises the National Press Building, where journalists from all over the world have their offices.

If you're in Georgetown, take a stroll through **Georgetown Park**. It's not a park but a shopping mall, one of the prettiest you'll ever see, nestled alongside the canal and featuring a marble fountain and glass skylight.

Washington, DC Convention & Tourism Corp.

Georgetown is a popular destination for shopping. There's no lack of trendy and upscale shops on Wisconsin Avenue and M Street. But beware: Other than the street vendors hawking jewelry and clothes, you won't find a lot of bargains.

Another place to shop in a nice setting is **Union Station**. This working train station houses 125 stores, lots of restaurants, and a nine-screen movie complex.

If big malls are more to your liking, the **Fashion Centre at Pentagon City** and the **Crystal City Shops** are relatively close by. For really big malls, you have to go farther outside the city. **Tysons Corner Center** in McLean, Virginia, is the largest in the area, with more than 290 stores. For outlet shopping, you'll have to travel farther to **Potomac Mills** in Prince William, Virginia.

On the Maryland side in Chevy Chase is the upscale **Chevy Chase Pavilion,** which offers food as well as shopping. And in Bethesda, Maryland, you'll find the more traditional but easy-to-navigate **Westfield Shoppingtown Montgomery** (also known as Montgomery Mall).

Is That All?

Are you ready for a different kind of fun? Why not try **DC Ducks** to tour D.C.? These tour buses turn into boats, so you get both a land and water tour on an authentic, fully restored 1942 "Duck."

If you prefer to pedal yourself, you can rent a paddleboat on the Tidal Basin. Or maybe you'd like to ride a carousel or see one of a number of shows. If you have the time, you could head to one of the amusement parks in the area. Just check ahead for schedules since they're only open seasonally.

Glen Echo Park

You don't have to go far to find a carousel. There's one right on the Mall, outside the Arts and Industries Building. But for an unusual treat, head to **Glen Echo Park,** a few miles northwest of the city, where you'll find one of only three hundred hand-carved wooden carousels still in existence. After a ride on the carousel, you can take in a puppet show at the Puppet Company or watch child actors bring fables and fairy tales to life at weekend performances by Adventure Theater. Next to the park is the **Clara Barton National Historic Site,** which honors the life and work of the person who established the American Red Cross.

Donna L. Barker

Enjoy the Show

Not far from Glen Echo Park in Bethesda is **Imagination Stage,** a family arts center that produces shows for kids year round.

Back downtown on the Mall, you'll find the smaller but very popular **Discovery Theater**. This theater hosts plays, storytellers, and puppet shows. Depending on the month, different themes may be explored such as Hispanic heritage, Native American life, and black history.

Test 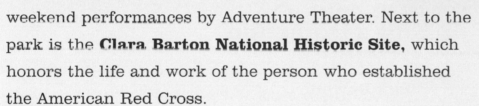 Yourself

Q: There is a lead, or "king" horse. Can you find it?

A: It's the largest one in the outside circle.

Q: The outside horses are called *standers*. Can you guess why?

A: They each have at least three feet on the ground.

Medieval Times

For a show where you can eat while you watch, you'll need to travel outside the city to Arundel Mills Mall in Hanover, Maryland. At the **Medieval Times Dinner and Tournament** you'll feast on an authentic four-course medieval meal during a live two-hour performance by knights on horseback. Remember to cheer on the knight whose section you're assigned to while you watch him compete in a thrilling contest of sport, using a variety of weapons.

King's Dominion

For an extra-big dose of entertainment, drive to **King's Dominion,** a 400-acre amusement park on the road to Richmond, Virginia, about eighty miles south of Washington. King's Dominion has four "launcher coasters," a new breed of coasters using compressed air to improve propulsion. The first is the popular Volcano Blaster Coaster, which snakes you in and out of a belching molten mountain at more than 70 MPH. Next is Flight of Fear, which features an enclosed track in semidarkness. The third is the Hypersonic XLC, which goes from 0 to 80 MPH in less than two seconds, catapulting riders 165 feet up—and down. The last is called the Italian Job Stunt Coaster.

There are nine other roller coasters at the park, as well as a water park, music and dance shows, and Paramount TV and movie characters.

Six Flags America

If you're really feeling wild and crazy, the best place to be is at **Six Flags America** in Largo, Maryland. This park features more than one hundred rides, slides, shows, and attractions, including state-of-the-art thrill rides, eight coasters, and Hurricane Harbor Water Park.

Try the ultra-fast megacoaster Superman: Ride of Steel, which soars two hundred feet into the air and races down a mile of track at 70 MPH. Or you can ride a spinning raft

Courtesy of Six Flags America

and do a triple-dip drop on the Penguin's Blizzard River. When you're ready for a break, you can relax at Buccaneer Beach, which has two pools, a pirate ship, water curtains, and slides.

Gulliver is lost in an amusement park. Help him find his way to the cotton candy.

Cotton Candy

FINISH

START

(Answer on page 149)

Got More Time?

Virginia

If you have an extra day or two, there are lots of sites worth visiting outside the Washington area. For example, America's "historical triangle"— Jamestown, Yorktown, and Williamsburg—is less than a three-hour drive southeast of the city in Virginia.

In 1607, thirteen years before the pilgrims landed in Massachusetts, Captain John Smith traveled to the banks of the James River and founded the **Jamestown Settlement**. It was the first English colony in the New World. For almost one hundred years these settlers fought the elements (and their enemies) to survive in this new land.

Jamestown Settlement offers the film *1607: A Nation Takes Root* as well as a large gallery with exhibits of archaeological artifacts from the seventeenth century. You can also visit re-creations of the ships the colonists used to travel to Virginia, try on English armor inside the fort, and grind some corn the way the Powhatan Indians did.

Photo courtesy of The Colonial Williamsburg Foundation, Williamsburg, VA

Did You Know?

About twenty minutes away by car, **Colonial Williamsburg** gives you an excellent in-depth understanding of the period of colonial life a few generations after the first settlers arrived in Jamestown. Beginning in 1699, for eighty-one years, Williamsburg was the political center of the largest colony (Virginia). Here the fundamental concepts of the republic were shaped by George Washington and Thomas Jefferson, among others. The movie *Story of a Patriot* is shown regularly at the Visitor's Center, and gives you a good feel for colonial life.

In the town of Williamsburg, each day different activities are highlighted so be sure to pick up a current brochure. Don't miss participating in the reenactment of a trial at the courthouse, watching the fife and drum march, or visiting the wig maker, the brick maker, the cooper, and the blacksmith. These and many other tradespeople spend their days hard at work, stopping to answer questions and to explain their trade in great detail. The colonial garden and the public jail—spelled "jaol" in those days— are also worth seeing. As you walk the streets of Williamsburg, you'll meet living actors playing members of the royalty, plantation owners, slaves, "redcoats," and the militia. If you want to take a carriage ride (for an additional fee), book early, as this popular attraction sells out quickly.

When you visit **Yorktown,** you'll see where the last major battle and siege of the American Revolution took place.

On October 19, 1781, the British surrendered to the combined American and French forces led by George Washington, ending the six-year war. This was the beginning of American independence.

The National Park Service offers tours of Yorktown Battlefield. Nearby, at the Yorktown Victory Center, you can visit a Continental Army encampment with sleeping quarters, supply tents, and cooking fires. You can participate in wooden musket drills or join the cannon crew. A visit to Yorktown offers a fascinating inside look at the end of Colonial America.

If you're ready for a break from American history, head over to **Busch Gardens Europe,** a beautifully landscaped theme park just a short ride from Williamsburg.

Busch Gardens has dozens of rides and attractions, ten major stage shows, and a magical children's area. The Griffon offers a 90-degree, 205-foot floorless dive, while the Curse of DarKastle is a castle frozen in time that might freeze you with fear! If you enjoy scary rides, this one's for you. If you prefer water parks, try **Water Country USA,** which offers state-of-the-art water rides and attractions set to a '50s and '60s surf theme. Both parks are open seasonally, so be sure to call ahead for schedules.

Did You Know?

The Continental forces—at 9,000—were in the minority during the Yorktown campaign. There were over 25,000 French army and navy men, and over 21,000 British army and navy men.

• • •

The term "powder room" came from the practice of a person going to a separate room to powder their wig. People thought a powdered wig gave them a more formal air.

Maryland

While Virginia offers plenty of history and entertainment, so does Washington's other neighboring state, Maryland.

Rose Hill Manor Park and Children's Museum is about an hour's drive from D.C., in Frederick. At this

George Grall, National Aquarium in Baltimore

refurbished former governor's mansion, you can play with toys from the 1800s and learn how to use old household tools. In the park, you'll see an icehouse, a log cabin, and a carriage museum with a wonderful display of sleighs.

The attractions in **Baltimore** could keep you busy for at least one full day. Your first stop should be the **National Aquarium in Baltimore,** which features more than 16,500 animals. Popular exhibits include Animal Planet Australia: Wild Extremes; Frogs! A Chorus of Colors; and the dolphin show *Play!*, which explores the dolphins' world of learning. Buy your tickets in advance and you'll avoid the long wait to get in.

If time allows, try some of the hands-on exhibits at the **Maryland Science Center**. **Port Discovery,** the children's museum in Baltimore, is also worth visiting, especially if you're traveling with younger kids. For an indoor/outdoor experience, go to the **Baltimore Maritime Museum,**

where you'll see the USS *Torsk* submarine, which sank the last two Japanese warships during World War II. Or if you'd rather stay outdoors, there's a nice selection of boat rides around the **Inner Harbor**. Prefer to eat and shop? Right on the harbor, you'll find two glass-enclosed pavilions called Harborplace with a huge selection of stores and restaurants.

Maryland's capital city, **Annapolis,** located on the Chesapeake Bay, is known as the "sailboat capital of the world." In the downtown Historic District, take a look at all the boats, from small sailboats to fancy yachts. And there are plenty of places to stop for a meal.

Not far away is the **United States Naval Academy**. Guided tours are available. Call in advance for reservations and security restrictions. Once on campus, you'll see the crypt of famous Revolutionary War hero John Paul Jones, a Mark XIV torpedo, and other Navy hardware.

Did You Know?

The United States Naval Academy has the world's largest dormitory, housing over 4,000 midshipmen.

West Virginia

Harpers Ferry, West Virginia (around one and a half hours from Washington by car), is located on the banks of the Potomac and Shenandoah rivers where Maryland, Virginia, and West Virginia meet. Harpers Ferry is most famous for a raid on the Armory conducted by abolitionist John

National Park Service

Did You Know?

Because Harpers Ferry is at the bottom of a ravine between two rivers and surrounded by mountains, Thomas Jefferson once said it was "perhaps one of the most stupendous scenes in nature."

Brown in 1859. (An abolitionist is a person who supported the end of the practice of slavery.) After the raid, Brown and his men were either captured or killed. Brown was tried for treason in the state of Virginia and hanged. Despite the failure of the raid, this event caught the attention of the whole country and helped incite the Civil War.

There are museums and exhibits in the town of Harpers Ferry, as well as hiking trails and park ranger–led tours.

For more information on these or any other of the places mentioned in this book, check the appendix for websites and phone numbers. Remember, the more advance planning you do, the more enjoyable your trip will be. Then once you're in town, call to double-check on the events you'd like to attend. Schedules can change without much notice.

Washington is a great place to visit. With all the museums, parks, historical homes, and memorials (not to mention restaurants and shops!), you'll expand your knowledge and have fun at the same time. Your visit to D.C. is bound to be one you'll never forget!

My Visit to Washington, D.C.

Recently, I had the chance to visit Washington, D.C., capital of _____ .
(name of country)

It was a really fun _____ . I went to lots of museums, including the
(noun)

_____ of _____ . My favorite exhibit was the one showing
(noun)   (noun)

the _____ with his jaws around the _____ . I also visited the
(animal)   (different animal)

_____ Memorial, which reminded me of _____ . I toured
(person's name)   (different person's name)

the _____ House, the Capitol, and the place our government
(adjective)

prints our _____ . But since I love _____ , my favorite place was
(noun)   (plural noun)

the _____ . There I was lucky enough to see the _____ _____ .
(noun)   (adjective)   (noun)

I ate lots of food in Washington, too, like _____ and _____ , which
(type of food)   (different type of food)

I don't normally eat in my hometown of _____ . To remember my
(name of city)

trip, I bought souvenirs, including a T-shirt that says _____ ,
(exclamation)

a _____ cap, and candy with _____ in it. Washington, D.C., is a
(adjective)   (plural noun)

great place to _____ . You should _____ there, too.
(verb)   (verb)

135

Appendix

African American Civil War Memorial and Museum
1000 and 1200 U St., NW
202-667-2667
www.afroamcivilwar.org

Albert Einstein Memorial/National Academy of Sciences
22nd and Constitution Aves., NW
202-334-2000
www.nasonline.org/site/PageServer

Annapolis and Anne Arundel County Conference and Visitors Bureau
Annapolis, MD
888-302-2852
www.visitannapolis.org

Arlington National Cemetery
West end of Memorial Bridge
Arlington, VA
703-607-8000
www.arlingtoncemetery.org

Baltimore Inner Harbor/Baltimore Area Convention and Visitors Association
Baltimore, MD
877-225-8466
www.baltimore.org/baltimore_inner_harbor.htm

Baltimore Maritime Museum
Piers 3 & 5, Baltimore's Inner Harbor
410-396-3453
www.baltomaritimemuseum.org

Brookside Nature Center
1400 Glenallan Ave.
Wheaton, MD
301-946-9071
www.mcparkandplanning.org/parks/facilities/
brookside_nature.shtm

Bureau of Engraving and Printing
14th and C Sts., SW
202-874-3019
www.moneyfactory.gov

Busch Gardens Europe
Busch Gardens Williamsburg
One Busch Gardens Blvd.
Williamsburg, VA
800-343-7946
www.buschgardens.com

Cabin John Park
7400 Tuckerman Lane
Rockville, MD
301-299-4555
www.mcparkandplanning.org/parks/facilities/regional_parks/
cabinjohn/index.shtm

C&O Canal
1057 Thomas Jefferson St., NW
202-653-5190
www.nps.gov/choh

Candy Cane City (Meadowbrook Park)
7901 Meadowbrook Lane
Chevy Chase, MD
www.mcparkandplanning.org/parks/park_of_the_day/jul/
parkday_jul26.shtm

Carroll County Farm Museum
500 South Center St.
Westminster, MD
410-386-3880
www.ccgov.carr.org/farm

The Castle (Smithsonian Building)
1000 Jefferson Dr., SW
202-633-1000
www.si.edu/visit/infocenter/sicastle.htm

Catoctin Wildlife Preserve and Zoo
13019 Catoctin Furnace Rd.
Thurmont, MD
301-271-3180
www.cwpzoo.com

Chevy Chase Pavilion
5335 Wisconsin Ave., NW
202-686-5335
www.ccpavilion.com

Clara Barton National Historic Site
5801 Oxford Rd.
Glen Echo, MD
 301-320-1410
www.nps.gov/clba

Claude Moore Colonial Farm at Turkey Run
6310 Georgetown Pike
McLean, VA
703-442-7557
www.1771.org

Colonial Williamsburg
Williamsburg, VA
800-HISTORY
www.colonialwilliamsburg.com

Corcoran Gallery of Art
500 17th St., NW
202-939-1700
www.corcoran.org

Croyden Creek Nature Center
852 Avery Rd.
Rockville, MD
240-314-8770
www.rockvillemd.gov/parks-facilities/croydon.htm

Crystal City Shops
Crystal Dr. between 15th and 23rd Sts.
Arlington, VA
703-922-4636
www.crystalcity.com/Dine_Shop_Stay

DC Ducks
Departs from:
Union Station, 50 Massachusetts Ave., NE
202-832-9800
www.historictours.com/washington/dcducks

D.C. United
RFK Stadium:
2400 East Capitol St., SE
202-675-5100
dcunited.mlsnet.com

Discovery Theater
Ripley Center
1100 Jefferson Dr., SW
202-357-1500
www.discoverytheater.org

Dumbarton Oaks
1703 32nd St., NW
202-339-6401
www.doaks.org

East Potomac Park
Ohio Dr., SW
south of Independence Ave. and the Tidal Basin
Golf Course: 202-554-7660
Golf Course: www.golfdc.com/gc/ep/gc.htm

Eastern Market
7th St. & North Carolina Ave., SE
www.easternmarket.net

ESPN Zone
555 12th St., NW
202-783-3776
www.espnzone.com/washingtondc

The Extra Mile—Points of Light Volunteer Pathway
15th St., NW, bordered by Pennsylvania Ave. and G St., NW
202-729-8165
www.extramile.us

Fashion Centre at Pentagon City
South Hayes St. and Army Navy Dr.
Arlington, VA
703-415-2400
www.simon.com/mall/default.aspx?ID=157

Ford's Theatre
511 10th St., NW
202-426-6924
www.fordstheatre.org

Franklin Delano Roosevelt Memorial
1850 W. Basin Dr., SW
202-426-6841
www.nps.gov/fdrm/home.htm

Frederick Douglass National Historic Site
1411 W St., SE
202-426-5961
www.nps.gov/frdo

Freer Gallery of Art and Arthur M. Sackler Gallery
Freer: 12th St. and Jefferson Dr., SW
Sackler: 1050 Independence Ave., SW
202-633-4800
www.asia.si.edu

Georgetown Park
3222 M St., NW
202-298-5577
www.shopsatgeorgetownpark.com

Georgetown University
37th and O Sts., NW
202-687-0100
www.georgetown.edu

Glen Echo Park
7300 MacArthur Blvd.
Glen Echo, MD
301-634-2222
glenechopark.org

Great Falls
11710 MacArthur Blvd.
Potomac, MD
301-299-3613
www.nps.gov/grfa

Hadley's Playground
12600 Falls Rd.
Potomac, MD
www.mcparkandplanning.org/parks/park_of_the_day/feb/
parkday_feb21.shtm

Harpers Ferry
Harpers Ferry, WV
304-535-6029
www.nps.gov/hafe/index.htm

Hirshhorn Museum and Sculpture Garden
7th St. and Independence Ave., SW
202-633-1000
www.hirshhorn.si.edu

Imagination Stage
4908 Auburn Ave.
Bethesda, MD
301-280-1660
www.imaginationstage.org

International Spy Museum
800 F St., NW
202-393-7798
www.spymuseum.org

Jamestown Settlement
Williamsburg, VA
888-593-4682
www.historyisfun.org/Jamestown-Settlement.htm

Jefferson Memorial
East Basin Dr., SW
202-426-6841
www.nps.gov/archive/thje/memorial/memorial.htm

John F. Kennedy Center for the Performing Arts
2700 F St., NW
202-467-4600
www.kennedy-center.org

Kenilworth Park and Aquatic Gardens
1900 Anacostia Dr., NE
202-426-6905
www.nps.gov/keaq

King's Dominion
16000 Theme Park Way
Doswell, VA
804-876-5000
www.paramountparks.com/kingsdominion/#actions

Korean War Veterans Memorial
French Dr., SW
202-426-6841
www.nps.gov/kwvm/home.htm

Library of Congress
101 Independence Ave., SE
202-707-8000
www.loc.gov/index.html

Lincoln Memorial
West Potomac Park at 23rd St., NW
202-426-6841
www.nps.gov/linc

Lincoln Museum
511 10th St., NW
202-426-6924
www.fordstheatre.org

Luray Caverns
970 U.S. Hwy. 211 West
Luray, VA
540-743-6551
www.luraycaverns.com

Marine Corps War Memorial
Arlington Blvd. and Meade St.
Arlington, VA
703-285-2601
www.nps.gov/archive/gwmp/usmc.htm

Martin Luther King Jr. National Memorial
East corner of Tidal Basin, National Mall
888-484-3373
www.mlkmemorial.org

Maryland Science Center
601 Light St.
Baltimore, MD
410-685-5225
www.mdsci.org

Medieval Times Dinner and Tournament
7000 Arundel Mills Circle
Hanover, MD
888-935-6878
www.medievaltimes.com

Metrobus/Metrorail
202-962-1234
www.wmata.com

Mitsitam
4th St. and Independence Ave., SW
202-275-2110
www.nmai.si.edu

Monticello
931 Thomas Jefferson Pkwy.
Charlottesville, VA
434-984-9822
www.monticello.org

Montrose Park
R St., NW
www.cr.nps.gov/nr/travel/wash/dc11.htm

Mount Vernon
3200 Mount Vernon Memorial Hwy.
Mount Vernon, VA
703-780-2000
www.mountvernon.org

Mount Zion Cemetery
27th and Q Sts., NW
202-234-0148
www.cr.nps.gov/nr/travel/wash/dc10.htm

NASA Goddard Space Flight Center
Soil Conservation Rd. and Explorer Dr.
Greenbelt, MD
301-286-9041
www.nasa.gov/centers/goddard/home

National Air and Space Museum
6th St. and Independence Ave., SW
202-633-1000
www.nasm.si.edu

National Air and Space Museum's Steven F. Udvar-Hazy Center
14390 Air and Space Museum Pkwy.
Chantilly, VA
202-633-1000
www.nasm.si.edu

National Aquarium
14th St. and Constitution Ave., NW
202-482-2825
www.nationalaquarium.com

National Aquarium in Baltimore
501 E Pratt St.
Baltimore, MD
410-576-3800
www.aqua.org

National Archives
Constitution Ave. between 7th and 9th Sts., NW
202-501-5000
www.archives.gov

National Building Museum
401 F St., NW
202-272-2448
www.nbm.org

National Colonial Farm
3400 Bryan Point Rd.
Accokeek, MD
301-283-2113
www.accokeek.org/visit/national_colonial_farm

National Gallery of Art and Sculpture Garden
Between 3rd and 9th Sts. at Constitution Ave., NW
202-737-4215
www.nga.gov

National Geographic Museum at Explorers Hall
1145 17th St., NW
202-857-7588
www.nationalgeographic.com/museum

National Japanese American Memorial
North of the Capitol on a plot bounded by Louisiana Ave., New Jersey Ave., and D St., NW
202-530-0015
www.njamf.com/welcome.htm

National Museum of African Art
950 Independence Ave., SW
202-633-4600
www.nmafa.si.edu

National Museum of American History
14th St. and Constitution Ave., NW
202-633-1000
www.americanhistory.si.edu

National Museum of Health and Medicine
6900 Georgia Ave., NW
202-782-2200
nmhm.washingtondc.museum

National Museum of Natural History
10th St. and Constitution Ave., NW
202-633-1000
www.mnh.si.edu

National Museum of the American Indian
4th St. and Independence Ave., SW
202-633-1000
www.nmai.si.edu

National Museum of the Marine Corps
18900 Jefferson Davis Hwy.
Triangle, VA
800-397-7585
www.usmcmuseum.org

National Museum of Women in the Arts
1250 New York Ave., NW
202-783-5000
www.nmwa.org

National Postal Museum
2 Massachusetts Ave., NE
202-633-5555
www.postalmuseum.si.edu

National World War II Memorial
900 Ohio Dr., SW
202-426-6841
www.nps.gov/nwwm

National Zoological Park
3001 Connecticut Ave., NW
202-633-4800
www.nationalzoo.si.edu

Oak Hill Cemetery
30th and R Sts., NW
www.cr.nps.gov/nr/travel/wash/dc9.htm

Old Post Office Pavilion
1100 Pennsylvania Ave., NW
202-289-4224
www.oldpostofficedc.com

Old Stone House
3051 M St., NW
202-895-6070
www.nps.gov/olst

Oxon Hill Farm
6411 Oxon Hill Rd.
Oxon Hill, MD
301-839-1176
www.nps.gov/archive/nace/oxhi/index.htm

Patuxent National Wildlife Visitor Center
12100 Beech Forest Rd.
Laurel, MD
301-497-5500
www.pwrc.usgs.gov

Pentagon
Army Navy Dr. and Fern St.
Arlington, VA
www.dtic.mil/ref/html/Welcome/general.html

Peterson House
516 10th St., NW
202-426-6924
www.fordstheatre.org

Port Discovery
35 Market Place
Baltimore, MD
410-727-8120
www.portdiscovery.org

Potomac Mills
2700 Potomac Mills Circle
Prince William, VA
703-496-9301
www.potomacmills.com/static/node752.jsp

Reston Zoo
1228 Hunter Mill Rd.
Vienna, VA
703-757-6222
www.restonzoo.com

Rock Creek Park Nature Center
5200 Glover Rd., NW
202-895-6070
www.nps.gov/archive/rocr/

Rose Hill Manor Park and Children's Museum
1611 North Market St.
Frederick, MD
301-694-1650
www.md-frederickcounty.civicplus.com/index.asp?nid=417

Sewall-Belmont House and Museum
Constitution Ave. and 2nd St., NE
202-546-1210
www.sewallbelmont.org

Shops at National Place
1331 Pennsylvania Ave., NW
202-662-1250

Six Flags America
13710 Central Ave.
Largo, MD
301-249-1500
www.sixflags.com/parks/America

Smithsonian American Art Museum and the National Portrait Gallery
8th and F Sts., NW
202-633-7970
www.AmericanArt.si.edu or www.npg.si.edu

Spy City Cafe
9th and F Sts., NW
202-654-0995
www.spymuseum.org/dine

Supreme Court of the United States
One 1st St., NE
202-479-3030
www.supremecourtus.gov

Tourmobile
202-554-5100
www.tourmobile.com

Tysons Corner Center
1961 Chain Bridge Road
McLean, VA
703-893-9400
www.shoptysons.com

Union Station
50 Massachusetts Ave., NE
202-289-1908
www.unionstationdc.com

United States Botanic Gardens
100 Maryland Ave., SW
202-225-8333
www.usbg.gov

United States Capitol
Capitol Hill at the east end of the Mall
202-224-3121
www.aoc.gov

United States Holocaust Memorial Museum
100 Raoul Wallenberg Pl., SW
202-488-0400
www.ushmm.org

United States National Arboretum
3501 New York Ave., NE
202-245-2726
www.usna.usda.gov

United States Naval Academy
Annapolis, MD
410-263-6933
www.usna.edu///homepage.php

U.S. Air Force Memorial
One Air Force Memorial Dr.
Arlington, VA
703-247-5808
www.airforcememorial.org

U.S. Navy Museum
Washington Navy Yard, Building 76
805 Kidder Breese, SE
202-433-4882
www.history.navy.mil

Verizon Center
601 F St., NW
202-628-3200
www.verizoncenter.com

Vietnam Veterans Memorial
Bacon Dr. and Constitution Ave., SW
202-426-6841
www.nps.gov/archive/vive/home.htm

Washington Capitals
Verizon Center: 601 F St., NW
202-628-3200
www.washingtoncaps.com

Washington Monument
15th St. and Constitution Ave., NW
202-426-6841
www.nps.gov/archive/wamo/home.htm

Washington Mystics
Verizon Center: 601 F St., NW
202-628-3200
www.wnba.com/mystics

Washington National Cathedral
3101 Wisconsin Ave., NW
202-537-6200
www.cathedral.org

Washington Nationals
RFK Stadium: 2400 East Capitol St., SE
202-675-5100
www.washington.nationals.mlb.com

Washington Redskins
FedEx Field: Raljon Rd.
Landover, MD
301-276-6050
www.redskins.com

Washington Wizards
Verizon Center: 601 F St., NW
202-628-3200
www.nba.com/wizards

Water Country USA
176 Water Country Pkwy.
Williamsburg, VA
800-343-7946
www.watercountryusa.com

Westfield Shoppingtown Montgomery
7101 Democracy Blvd.
Bethesda, MD
301-469-6025
www.westfield.com/montgomery

Wheaton Regional Park
2000 Shorefield Rd.
Wheaton, MD
301-942-6703
www.mcparkandplanning.org/parks/facilities/regional_parks/
wheaton/index.shtm

White House and Visitor's Center
1600 Pennsylvania Ave., NW
202-456-2121
www.whitehouse.gov

Woodrow Wilson House
2340 S St., NW
202-387-4062
www.woodrowwilsonhouse.org

Yorktown
Yorktown, VA
757-898-2410
www.nps.gov/archive/colo/Yorktown/ythome

Car Games

Long car rides don't have to be boring or drive you crazy. Playing games will make the time fly. You don't have to sit still and get sore, stiff, and restless either. Stretch out and move your tired muscles with some easy car exercises. They'll keep you from wishing you could roll down the window and scream or kick open the door and jump out.

Games are for fun, so laugh it up and play the ride away.

Things to take along on any long ride:
• something hard and flat to write on—like a tray, board, or large hardcover book
• coloring pens, pencils, or crayons
• pad of paper or notebook
• deck of cards
• books to read

Word Games

Think of as many names as you can for each letter of the alphabet. *D*: Debbie, Doug, Diane, Denise, Dan, and so on.

Look for each letter of the alphabet on car license plates as they pass (you can skip the hard-to-find letters *Q* and *Z*).

Make words out of the letters you see on car license plates. For example: 125 BHV, say *beehive*.

Packing for your trip: Name things you can put in your suitcase starting with the letter *A*, then *B*, then C, and so on. For example: Apple, Baseball, Cat, Dictionary (they don't really *have* to be things you need on your trip).

Counting Games

Watch car license plates and count the numbers, starting with zero. See who can reach nine first. Or keep counting to twenty—it takes longer.

Find the most: Pick something to count and see who can find the most. You can pick things like green cars, stop signs, license plates from Washington, D.C., people driving with hats on, kids in cars, and so on.

Guessing Games

Twenty Questions: Think of something for the others to guess. They ask you questions to try to figure out what it is. You can only answer "yes" or "no." If no one guesses in twenty questions, you win. Or you can just let them keep asking questions until someone figures it out.

Pictionary (like dictionary, but with pictures): Like Twenty Questions, someone is "it" and thinks of something that everyone else tries to guess. You draw pictures for them to give them clues and hints—but you can't draw what the answer is. You could pick the name of your school. Then, for clues, you could draw your classroom, desk, schoolbook, lunch box, or teacher—or anything else you might think of. Draw pictures until someone guesses what it is you're thinking of.

Drawing

One person draws a mark, line, shape, letter, or number, and someone else has to make a picture out of it.

Stories

One person starts to make up a story. The next person has to add the next line or sentence to the story; then on to the next person. Everyone in the car takes a turn making up the story line-by-line. It can turn out to be a pretty funny story. You might even end up on the moon with a _____.

Make up a travel friend: This is your chance to say anything you want about your trip. You pretend that you have an invisible friend taking the trip with you. Only you can see and hear your friend, so you have to tell everyone else what your friend is saying. Does he or she like your car? Where does she want to go tomorrow? What does he like to eat? You can say ANYTHING. Make up a story about where your friend is from, what his or her family is like—or whatever you want.

Cards

Bring along a deck of cards and play your favorite games. Or, if there's room, you can turn a hat over and try to toss the cards into it. You have to throw them as if they were tiny Frisbees.

Movement Games

Charades: Someone acts out a kind of animal (or anything else) using only face and hands. Everyone else has to guess what she or he is.

Simon Says: Someone is Simon. Everyone else has to do whatever Simon says—but only when Simon says, "Simon says. . . ." If Simon doesn't say this and you do what he or she says, you goof. Like this: "Simon says, 'Touch your nose with your right hand.'" (Simon touches his nose. Everyone else does, too.) Simon gives lots of directions, then he sneaks in an order without saying "Simon says" but does it anyway. If anyone follows, he or she goofs.

Statue: Everyone playing this game freezes into a statue. See who can stay that way the longest without moving.

Making Faces: Someone is "it." He or she makes a face—sad, goofy, happy, sleepy, cranky—and the other person has to imitate the face. This simple game is really a crack-up.

Exercises

You'll be amazed at how much exercise you can get while riding in a car. You can't swim, run, or throw a ball, but you can work out by stretching your muscles. Make up your own stretches, or do the ones in the following paragraph. Remember to hold one stretch to the count of ten before beginning another. And don't forget to take a deep breath and blow it out slowly with every stretch. It's "car yoga."

Touch your toes. Stretch your arms straight out. Spin them in circles. Twist around as far as you can. Reach for the ceiling. Bend your head back. Bend it forward. Press your hands down on the seat next to you and try to lift yourself off the seat. Flex your feet up, then down; point your toes. Repeat this ten times. You'll be surprised at how good this feels for stiff muscles.

Answers to Puzzles

page 21
4 blocks

page 29

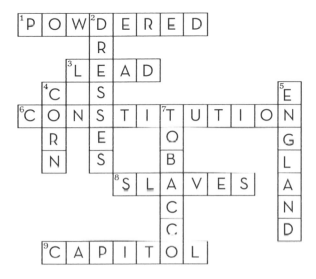

page 35
1. John and Abigail Adams, November 1800
2. Grover Cleveland; June 2, 1886
3. Ronald Reagan broadcast for the Chicago Cubs in the mid-1930s
4. John Quincy Adams
5. Theodore Roosevelt

page 36

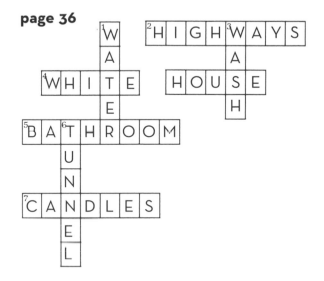

page 46
Declaration of Independence
    Men, Equal, Rights, Liberty

Constitution
    United States, Justice, Welfare, America

Bill of Rights
    Religion, Speech, Press

page 64
1. Jefferson Memorial
2. Washington Monument
3. Lincoln Memorial
4. Capitol
5. White House
6. Marine Corps War Memorial

page 77

Mercury
Venus
Earth
Mars
Jupiter
Saturn
Uranus
Neptune

page 106

page 103

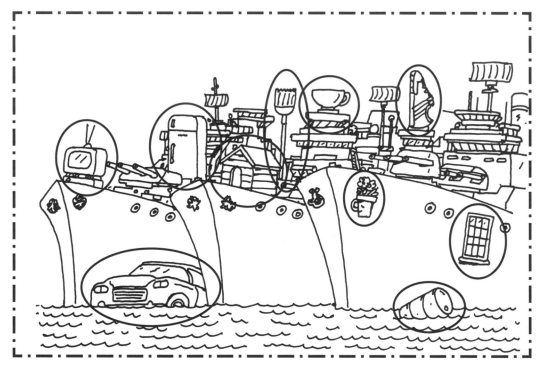

page 112

ANTELOPE   NIGHTINGALE

BABOON   OWL

CHEETAH   PANDA

DEER   QUAIL

ELEPHANT   RACCOON

FOX   SQUIRREL

GIRAFFE   TIGER

HYENA   UNICORN

IGUANA   VAMPIRE BAT

JAGUAR   WOLF

KANGAROO   X

LEOPARD   YAK

MOUSE   ZEBRA

page 128

Index